ESTATE PUBLICATIONS

KENT

KU-545-728

Street maps with index
Administrative Districts
Population Gazetteer
Road Map with index
Postcodes

COUNTY RED BOOKS

This atlas is intended for those requiring street maps of the historical and commercial centres of towns within the county. Each locality is normally presented on one or two pages and although, with many small towns, this space is sufficient to portray the whole urban area, the maps of large towns and cities are for centres only and are not intended to be comprehensive. Such coverage is offered in Super and Local Red Books (see page 2).

Every effort has been made to verify the accuracy of information in this Atlas but the Publishers cannot accept responsibility for expense or loss caused by any error or omission. Any information that would improve the usefullness of these maps will be welcomed.

The representation on these maps of a road, track or path is no evidence of the exictence of a right of way.

Street plans prepared and published by ESTATE PUBLICATIONS, Bridewell House, TENTERDEN, KENT, and based upon the ORDNANCE SURVEY mapping with the permission of The Controller of H. M. Stationery Office.

The Publishers acknowledge the co-operation of the local authorities of towns represented in this atlas.

Estate Publications   30 M   ISBN 0 86084 765 9   © Crown Copyright 398713

COUNTY RED BOOK

KENT

contains street maps for each town centre

SUPER & LOCAL RED BOOKS

are street atlases with comprehensive local coverage

ASHFORD & TENTERDEN
including: Charing, St. Michaels, Wye etc.

BROMLEY
including: Beckenham, Chelsfield, Chislehurst, Farnborough, Orpington etc.

FOLKESTONE & DOVER
including: Aylesham, Cheriton, Deal, Dymchurch, Eastry, Hythe, New Romney, Walmer etc.

GRAVESEND & DARTFORD
including: Greenhithe, Hartley, Meopham, New Ash Green, Swanley, Swanscombe etc.

MAIDSTONE
including: Bearsted, Ditton, Headcorn, Snodland, Staplehurst etc.

MEDWAY & GILLINGHAM
including: Chatham, Hoo, Rainham, Rochester, Walderslade etc.

SEVENOAKS
including: Borough Green, Kemsing, Westerham, West Kingsdown etc.

SITTINGBOURNE & FAVERSHAM
including: Leysdown on Sea, Minster, Queenborough, Sheerness etc.

THANET & CANTERBURY
including: Herne Bay, Margate, Minster, Ramsgate, Sandwich, Whitstable etc.

TUNBRIDGE WELLS & TONBRIDGE
including: Cranbrook, Crowborough, Edenbridge, Hadlow, Hawkhurst, Paddock Wood, Southborough, Wadhurst etc.

CONTENTS

LEGEND TO STREET PLANS

One-way street	⟶	Post Office	●
Pedestrianized	▨	Public Convenience	Ⓒ
Car Park	🅿	Place of worship	✚

4 ADMINISTRATIVE DISTRICTS

GAZETTEER INDEX TO ROAD MAPS
with populations

County of Kent population   1,508,873

Districts:

Ashford	92,331	Rochester upon Medway	144,870
Canterbury	123,947	Sevenoaks	108,828
Dartford	79,439	Shepway	91,486
Dover	103,216	Swale	115,769
Gillingham	95,358	Thanet	123,665
Gravesham	92,454	Tonbridge & Malling	101,763
Maidstone	132,209	Tunbridge Wells	99,538

Acol 279	11 G2	Charing Heath	10 B4	Five Oak Green	9 F5
Acrise 168	*	Chartham 2,942	10 D3	Folkestone 45,280	11 F6
Addington 644	9 F3	Chartham Hatch	10 D3	Fordcombe	8 D6
Adisham 645	11 F4	Chart Sutton 813	9 G5	Fordwich 295	11 E3
Aldington 1,011	10 D6	Chatham. 22,395		Four Elms	8 C5
Alkham 607	11 F5	Chattenden	9 G2	Four Throws	12 D2
Allhallows 1,767	9 H1	Cheeseman's Green	10 D6	Frindsbury Extra 5,093	9 F2
Appledore 669	13 F2	Chestfield 2,725	11 E2	Frinsted 154	10 B3
Ash 2,707	11 G3	Chevening 2,905	8 D3	Frittenden 885	9 G6
Ash cum Ridley 7,575	9 E3	Chiddingstone 1,122	8 D5		
Ashford 43,348	10 C5	Chiddingstone Causeway	8 D5	Gillingham 95,358	9 G2
Ashurst	8 D6	Chilham 1,556	10 D4	Godmersham 338	10 D4
Aylesford 9,506	9 G3	Chillenden	11 F4	Golden Green	9 E5
Aylesham 4,044	11 F4	Chipstead	8 D4	Goodnestone (nr. Canterbury) 365	11 F3
		Chislet 812	11 F2	Goodnestone with Graveney 432	10 D3
Badger's Mount	8 D3	Claygate Cross	9 E4	Goudhurst 2,498	9 F6
Badlesmere 117	10 C4	Cliffe 5,271	9 G1	Grafty Green	10 B4
Bapchild 946	10 B3	Cliffsend	11 G2	Grain	9 H1
Barfreston	11 F4	Cliftonville	11 H1	Graveney with Goodnestone 432	10 D3
Barham 1,254	11 F4	Cobham 1,359	9 F2	Gravesend 50,741	9 F1
Barming 1,724	9 F4	Coldred with Shepherdswell 1,810	11 F4	Great Chart with Singleton 2,557	10 C5
Bean 1,768	9 E2	Collier Street	9 F5	Great Mongeham	11 G4
Bearsted 7,841	9 G4	Collier's Green	9 G6	Great Stonar	11 G3
Bekesbourne with Patrixbourne 788	11 E3	Conyer	10 C2	Greatstone-on Sea	13 H3
Benenden 1,727	12 D2	Cooling 157	9 G1	Greenhithe & Swanscombe 9.348	9 E1
Benover	9 F5	Cowden 743	8 C6	Grove	11 F3
Bethersden 1,341	10 B5	Coxheath 3,954	9 G4	Guston 1,662	11 G5
Betsham	9 E2	Cranbrook 5,840	9 G6		
Betteshanger	11 G4	Crockenhill 1,615	8 D2	Hackington 577	*
Bicknor 63	10 B3	Crockham Hill	8 C4	Hadlow 3,560	9 E4
Bidborough 967	9 E5	Crundale 175	10 D4	Haffenden Quarter	10 B5
Biddenden 2,205	10 A6	Culverstone Green	9 E3	Hale Street	9 F4
Bilsington 310	13 G2	Curtisden Green	9 G6	Halfway	10 B1
Bilting	10 D4	Cuxton 2,742	9 F2	Halling 1,985	9 F3
Birchington 9,859	11 G2			Halstead 1,643	8 D3
Birling 383	9 F3	Darenth 3,894	9 E2	Ham	11 G4
Bishopsbourne 243	11 E4	Dargate	10 D3	Hamstreet	13 G2
Blean 1,708	11 E3	Dartford 44,817	8 D2	Harbledown 2,055	11 E3
Bluebell Hill	9 G3	Deal 28,504˙	11 G4	Harrietsham 1,352	10 B4
Bobbing 1,544	10 B2	Deᵣisole	11 F5	Hartley (nr Cranbrook)	12 D1
Bonnington 119	10 D6	Denton with Wootton 356	11 F4	Harley (nr Dartford) 5,655	9 E2
Borden 2,094	10 B3	Derringstone	11 F4	Hartlip 677	10 A2
Borough Green 3,253	9 E4	Detling 781	9 G3	Hassell Street	10 D5
Bossingham	11 G4	Ditton 4,854	9 F3	Hastingleigh 212	10 D5
Boughton Aluph 587	10 D4	Doddington 541	10 B3	Hawkenbury	9 G5
Boughton Green	9 G4	Dover 37,826	11 G5	Hawkhurst 4,217	12 D2
Boughton Lees	10 C4	Downswood 2,389	*	Hawkinge 2,224	11 F5
Boughton Malherbe 453	10 B4	Dunkirk 1,149	10 D3	Headcorn 3,058	10 A5
Boughton Monchelsea 1,704	*	Dunk's Green	9 E4	Heaverham	9 E3
Boughton Street 1,929	10 D2	Dunton Green 1,563	8 D3	Herne	11 E2
Boxley 8,558	9 G3	Dymchurch 3,360	13 H2	Herne Bay 32,773	11 E2
Boyden Gate	11 F2			Hernhill 576	10 D3
Brabourne 1,363	10 D5	Eastchurch 1,548	10 C1	Hersden	11 F3
Brabourne Lees	10 D5	East End	10 A6	Hever 1,077	8 D5
Brasted 1,374	8 C4	East Farleigh 1,300	9 G4	Hextable	8 D2
Brasted Chart	8 C4	East Langdon	11 G5	Higham 3,911	9 F2
Bredgar 632	10 B3	East Malling, (inc. Larkfield) 12,124	9 F4	High Halden 1,411	10 B6
Bredhurst 404	9 G3	East Peckham 3,387	9 F5	High Halstow. 1,288	9 G1
Brenchley 1,756	9 F5	East Studdal	11 G4	Highsted	10 B3
Brenzett 345	13 G2	East Sutton 301	*	Hildenborough 4,849	9 E5
Bridge 2,493	11 E4	Eastling 360	10 C3	Hillborough	11 E2
British Legion Village	9 F3	Eastry 2,273	11 G3	Hinxhill with Wye 1,996	10 D5
Broadoak	11 E3	Eastwell 121	*	Hoaden	11 F3
Broadstairs 23,691	11 H2	Eccles	9 F3	Hoath 514	11 F2
Brompton	9 G2	Edenbridge 7,581	8 C5	Hollingbourne 949	10 A4
Brook 339	10 D5	Egerton 945	10 B4	Honey Hill	11 E3
Brookland 469	13 F3	Elham 1,429	11 E5	Hoo St. Werburgh 7,279	9 G2
Broomfield (nr. Herne Bay)	11 E2	Elmsted Court 251	11 E5	Horsmonden 1,981	9 F6
Broomfield (nr Maidstone) 1,703	10 A4	Elmstone	11 F3	Horton Kirby & South Darenth 3,019	9 E2
Buckland 83	11 G5	Elvington	11 F4	Hothfield 887	10 C5
Burham 1,254	9 F3	Etchinghill	11 E5	Hougham without 414	*
Burmarsh 326	13 H2	Ewell Minnis	11 F5	Hucking 61	9 H3
		Eyhorne Street	9 H4	Hunton 603	9 F4
Canterbury 38,670	11 E3	Eynsford 1,772	8 D2	Hythe 13,751	11 E6
Capel 2,208	*	Eythorne 2,467	11 F4		
Capel le Ferne 1,998	11 F5			Ickham 398	11 F3
Chainhurst	9 F5	Fairseat	9 E3	Ide Hill	8 D4
Chalk	9 F2	Farningham 1,365	8 D2	Iden Green	12 D2
Challock Lees 746	10 C4	Faversham 17,070	10 C3	Ightham 1,743	9 E4
Charing. 2,707	10 C4	Fawkham Green 509	9 E2	Isle of Grain 1,775	9 H1

Place	Grid Ref
Ivychurch 169	13 G2
Ivy Hatch	9 E4
Iwade 934	10 B2
Kemsing 3,942	8 D3
Kenardington 244	13 F2
Kennington	10 C5
Kilndown	9 F6
Kingsdown with Ringwould 1,951	11 H4
Kingsnorth 2,627	10 C5
Kingston 493	11 E4
Kingswood	10 A4
Knockholt 1,186	8 C3
Knockholt Pound	8 D3
Knowlton	11 F4
Laddingford	9 F5
Lamberhurst 1,394	9 F6
Langdon 564	*
Langley 1,176	9 G4
Langton Green	8 D6
Leaveland 113	10 C4
Leeds 774	9 H4
Leigh 1,518	8 D5
Leigh Green	13 E2
Lenham 3,103	10 B4
Lenham Heath	10 B4
Leybourne 2,940	9 F3
Leysdown-on-Sea 1,057	10 D2
Linton 529	9 G4
Littlebourne 1,417	11 F3
Little Chart 237	10 C5
Littlestone on Sea	13 H3
Longfield & New Barn 4,909	9 E2
Loose 2,369	9 G4
Lower Halstow 1,283	10 B2
Lower Hardres 532	11 E4
Lower Higham	9 F2
Luddenham 109	*
Luddesdown 227	9 F2
Luton	9 G2
Lydd 5,309	13 G3
Lydden 693	11 F5
Lydd on Sea	13 H3
Lymbridge Green	11 E5
Lyminge 2,455	11 E5
Lympne 1,221	13 H1
Lynsted 891	10 C3
Maidstone 71,200	9 G4
Maltman's Hill	10 B5
Manston 424	*
Marden 3,648	9 G5
Margate 38,535	11 G2
Markbeech	8 D5
Marlpit Hill	8 C5
Marshborough	11 C3
Marsh Green	8 C5
Matfield	9 F5
Meopham 8,864	9 E2
Mereworth 1,246	9 F4
Mersham 1,046	10 D5
Milebush	9 G5
Milstead & Kingsdown 290	10 B3
Milton Regis	10 B2
Minnis Bay	11 G2
Minster in Sheppey	10 C1
Minster (Thanet) 3,286	11 G2
Molash 238	10 D4
Monks Horton 113	*
Monkton 662	*
Nackington	11 E4
Nettlestead 869	9 F4
Netlestead Green	9 F4
New Ash Green	9 E2
Newchurch 307	13 G2
Newenden 201	13 E2
New Hythe	9 F3
Newington (nr Hythe) 307	11 E6
Newington (nr Rainham 2,454	10 B2
Newnham 361	10 C3
New Romney 6,204	13 G3
Nonington 665	11 F4
Northbourne 766	11 G4
Northfleet 21,389	9 E1
Norton 323	*
Oad Street	10 B3
Oare 530	10 C3
Offham 402	9 F4
Old Romney 194	13 G3
Old Wives Lees	10 D4
Orlestone 1,189	13 G1
Ospringe 598	10 C3
Otford 3,282	8 D3
Otham 399	9 G4
Otterden 163	*
Paddlesworth 42	11 E5
Paddock Wood 7,141	9 F5
Patrixbourne with Bekesbourne 788	11 E3
Pembury 6,016	9 E6
Penshurst 1,509	8 D5
Petham 668	11 E4
Platt 1,339	9 E4
Plaxtol 280	9 E4
Pluckley 88	10 B5
Postling 185	11 E6
Preston 672	11 F3
Queenborough 3,689	*
Rainham	9 G3
Ram Lane	10 C5
Ramsgate 38,095	11 H2
Reading Street	13 F2
Reculver	11 F2
Redbrook Street	10 B6
Rhodes Minnis	11 E5
Ringwould with Kingsdown 1,951	11 G4
Ripple 368	11 G4
Riverhead 1,883	8 D4
Rochester 26,971	9 G2
Rodmersham 539	10 B3
Rolvenden 1,440	13 E2
Rolvenden Layne	13 E2
Rough Common	11 E3
Ruckinge 739	13 G2
Ryarsh 1,095	9 F3
St Margaret's-at-Cliffe 2,415	11 G5
St Mary-in-the-Marsh 363	13 G2
St Mary's Bay	13 H2
St Mary's Hoo 187	9 G1
St Michael's	10 B6
St Nicholas-at-Wade 773	11 F2
St Peter's	11 G2
Saltwood 818	11 E6
Sandgate	11 F6
Sandhurst 1,302	12 D2
Sandling	9 G4
Sandwich 4,729	11 G3
Sarre 101	11 F2
Seal 2,300	8 D4
Seasalter	10 D2
Sellindge 1,319	10 D6
Selling 687	10 D3
Sevenoaks 18,130	8 D4
Sevenoaks Weald 1,201	8 D4
Sevington 214	10 C5
Shadoxhurst 1,048	10 C6
Sheerness 12,090	10 B1
Sheldwich 456	10 B1
Shepherdswell with Coldred 1,810	11 F4
Shepway	9 G4
Shipbourne 1,129	9 E4
Sholden 815	11 G4
Shoreham 2,023	*
Shorne 2,186	9 F2
Shottenden	10 D4
Sissinghurst	9 G6
Sittingbourne 36,630	10 B2
Small Hythe	13 E2
Smarden 1,144	10 B5
Smarden Bell	10 B5
Smeeth 864	10 D5
Snargate 92	13 F2
Snave	13 G2
Snodland 8,814	9 F3
Solestreet	10 D4
Southborough 10,730	9 E5
South Darenth & Horton Kirby 3,019	9 E2
Southfleet 1,251	9 E2
Speldhurst 4,731	8 D5
Stalisfield Green 204	10 C4
Standen	10 B5
Stanford 456	11 E6
Stanhope 4,024	*
Stansted 850	9 E3
Staple 467	11 F3
Staplehurst 5,786	9 G5
Stelling Minnis 568	11 E4
Stockbury 673	9 H3
Stodmarsh	11 F3
Stoke 1,030	9 H1
Stone (in Oxney) 347	13 F2
Stone (in Dartford) 7,060	9 E1
Stourmouth 251	11 F3
Stowting 228	11 E5
Strood	9 F2
Sturry 6,285	11 E3
Sundridge 1,847	8 D4
Sutton 829	11 G4
Sutton-at-Hone & Hawley 4,103	8 D2
Sutton Valence 1,374	9 G5
Swalecliffe	11 E2
Swanley 21,081	8 D2
Swanscombe, & Greenhithe 9,348	9 E1
Swingfield Minnis 1,142	11 F5
Tankerton	11 E2
Temple Ewell 1,797	11 F5
Tenterden 7,005	13 E2
Teston 630	9 F4
Teynham 2,945	10 C3
Thanington without 6,519	11 E3
The Forstal	10 B5
The Moor	12 D2
Thong	9 F2
Three Chimneys	10 A6
Throwley 292	10 C3
Thurnham 889	9 G4
Tilmanstone 375	11 G4
Tonbridge 30,358	9 E5
Tonge 302	*
Tovil 2,713	9 G4
Toy's Hill	8 C4
Trottiscliffe 514	9 E3
Tudeley	9 E5
Tunbridge Wells 55,145	9 E6
Tunstall 850	10 B3
Tyler Hill	11 E3
Ulcombe 854	10 A4
Under Riven	8 D4
Upchurch 1,953	9 H2
Uplees	10 C2
Upnor	9 G2
Upper Hardres 390	*
Wainscott	9 G2
Walderslade	9 G3
Wallend	9 H1
Walmer	11 G4
Waltham 397	10 D4
Warden 1,426	10 C1
Warehorne 306	13 F2
Warren Street	10 B4
Wateringbury 1,720	9 F4
Well Hill	8 D3
West Cliffe	11 G5
West Farleigh 430	9 F4
West Hougham	11 F5
West Kingsdown 5,460	8 D3
West Malling 2,506	9 F4
West Langdon	11 G4
West Peckham 317	9 E4
West Street	10 B4
Westbere 375	11 E3
Westerham 3,948	8 C4
Westgate-on-Sea	11 G2
Westmarsh	11 F3
Westwell 717	10 C4
Westwell Leacon	10 C4
Whetsted	9 F5
Whitfield 4,579	11 G5
Whitley Row	8 D4
Whitstable 29,485	10 D2
Wichling 131	10 B3
Wickhambreux 474	11 F3
Wigmore	9 G3
Willesborough	10 D5
Wilmington 6,743	8 D2
Wilsley Pound	9 G6
Wingham 1,553	11 F3
Wittersham 1,084	13 E2
Womenswold 319	11 F4
Woodchurch 1,781	13 F2
Woodnesborough 985	11 G3
Woolage Green	11 F4
Wootton with Denton 356	11 F5
Wormshill 231	10 B3
Worth 886	11 G3
Wouldham 938	9 F3
Wrotham 1,767	9 E3
Wye with Hinxhill 1,996	10 D5
Yalding 2,816	9 F4
Yorkletts	10 D3

Population figures are based upon the 1991 census and relate to the local authority ward or parish, as constituted at that date. Boundaries of the districts are shown on pages 4-5. Places with no population figure form part of a larger local authority area or parish.

Population figures in bold type

* Place not included on map pages 8-13 due to limitation of space.

7

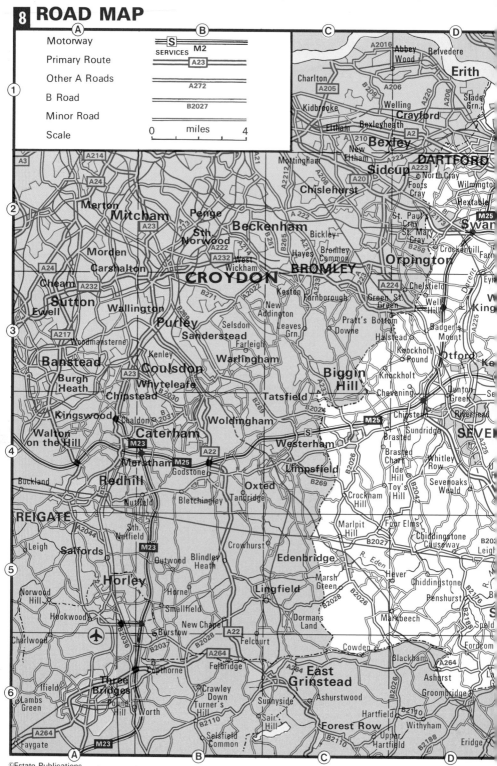

8 ROAD MAP

Motorway
Primary Route
Other A Roads
B Road
Minor Road
Scale

M2
SERVICES
A23
A272
B2027
0 miles 4

©Estate Publications

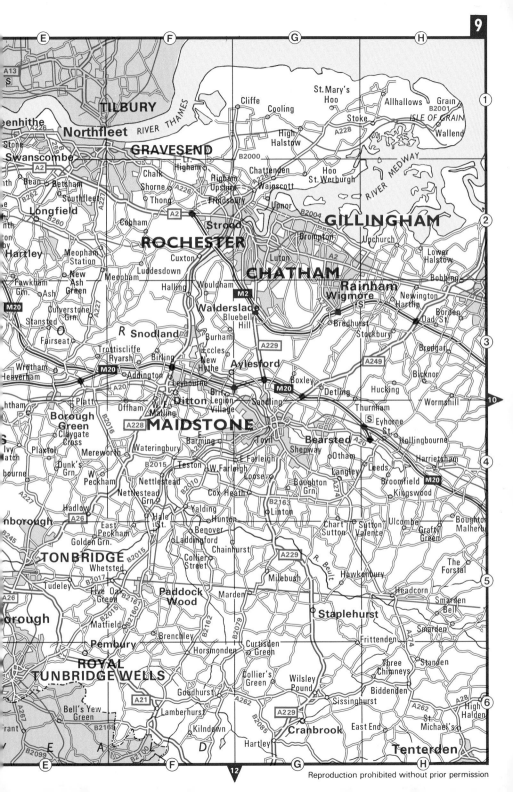

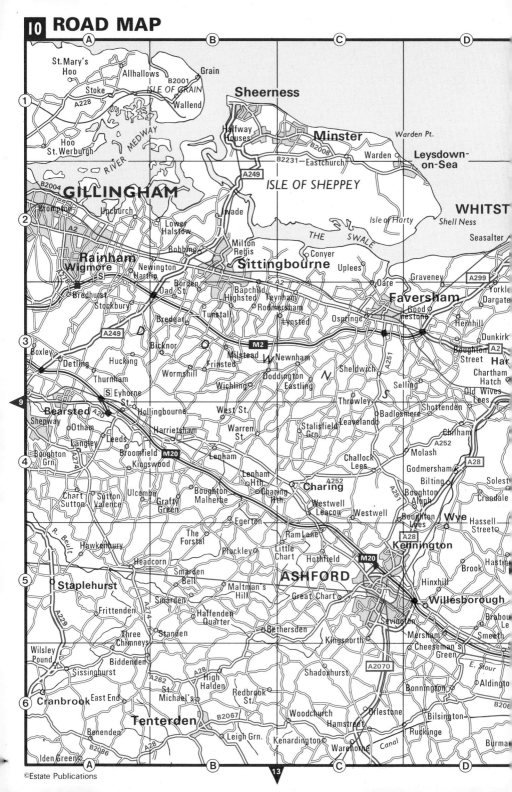

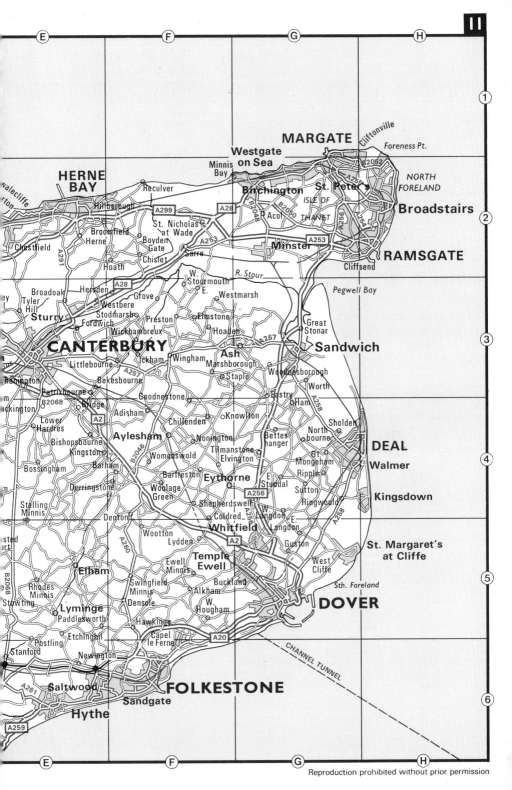

E F G H

1

MARGATE
Cliftonville
Foreness Pt.
Westgate
Minnis on Sea
Bay
NORTH
FORELAND
HERNE
BAY
Reculver
Birchington
St. Peter's
Hillborough
A299
A28
B2048
B2050
ISLE OF
THANET
Acol
Broadstairs
B2052
A255
A256
2
St. Nicholas
at Wade
Broomfield
Herne
Boyden
Gate
A253
Chestfield
Minster
A253
RAMSGATE
Chislet
Sarre
Hoath
Cliffsend
A291
W.
Stourmouth
R. Stour
Pegwell Bay
Broadoak
Hersden
A28
E.
Westmarsh
Tyler
Hill
Grove
Westbere
Stodmarsh
Preston
Elmstone
Great
Stonar
3
Sturry
Fordwich
Wickhambreux
Hoaden
CANTERBURY
Ash
Sandwich
Littlebourne
ckham
Wingham
Marshborough
Woodnesborough
Bekesbourne
Staple
Worth
Patrixbourne
Goodnestone
Eastry
Ham
A257
B2068
Bridge
Adisham
Knowlton
A568
Lower
Hardres
A2
Chillenden
North
bourne
Sholden
Bishopsbourne
Kingston
Nonington
Bettes
hanger
Gt
Mongeham
DEAL
4
Bossingham
Barham
Womenswold
Tilmanstone
Elvington
Ripple
Walmer
Derringstone
Woolage
Green
Barfreston
Eythorne
E
Studdal
Sutton
Ringwould
Kingsdown
Stelling
Minnis
Denton
Shepherdswell
Coldred
Langdon
E.
Langdon
Whitfield
A256
St. Margaret's
at Cliffe
sted
rt
Wootton
Lydden
A2
Guston
Temple
Ewell
West
Cliffe
5
Elham
Ewell
Minnis
Sth. Foreland
Swingfield
Minnis
Buckland
Rhodes
Minnis
Densole
Alkham
W.
Hougham
Stowting
Lyminge
Paddlesworth
Hawkinge
DOVER
Etchinghil
Capel
le Ferne
Postling
A20
CHANNEL TUNNEL
Stanford
Newington
6
Saltwood
FOLKESTONE
A261
Sandgate
Hythe
A259

E F G H

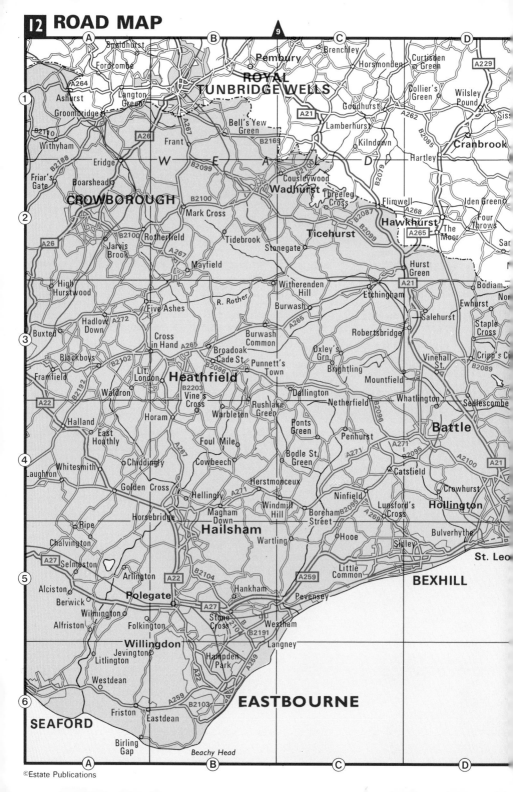

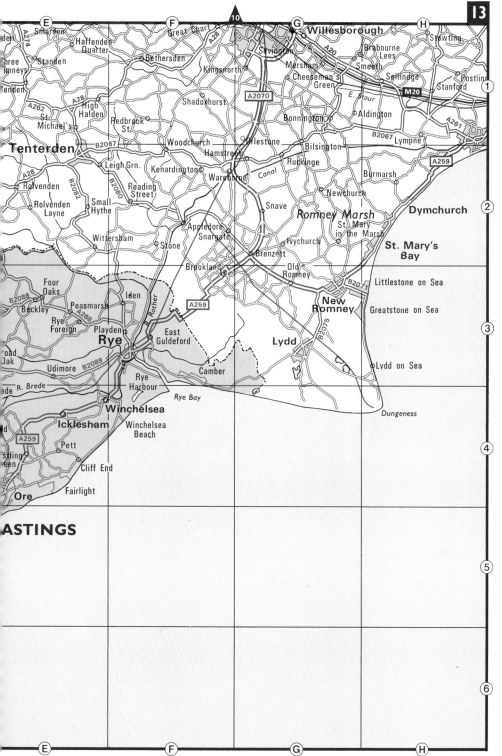

10

E   F   G Willesborough   H

Smarden
Haffenden
Quarter
A274
den
Standen
hree
mneys
enden
A262
St.
Michael's
High
Halden
A28
Redbrook
St.
Tenterden
Rolvenden
B2082
Rolvenden
Layne
Small
Hythe
B2080
Reading
Street
Leigh Grn.
Kenardington
Four
Oaks
B2088
Beckley
Peasmarsh
A268
Rye
Foreign
Playden
Rye
oad
Oak
Udimore
B2089
ede R. Brede
Winchelsea
Icklesham
A259
Pett
d
Cliff End
Ore
Fairlight

ASTINGS

Great Chart
A28
Bethersden
Kingsnorth
Shadoxhurst
A2070
Woodchurch
Hamstreet
Warehorne
Appledore
Snargate
Stone
Brookland
Iden
Rother
A259
East
Guldeford
Camber
Rye
Harbour
Winchelsea
Beach

Sevington
Mersham
Cheeseman's
Green
Bonnington
Orlestone
Bilsington
Ruckinge
Canal
Snave
Ivychurch
Brenzett
Old
Romney
A20
Brabourne
Lees
Smeeth
Sellindge
E. Stour
Aldington
B2067 Lympne
A259
Burmarsh
Newchurch
Romney Marsh
St. Mary
in the Marsh
New
Romney
B2071
B2075
Lydd
Littlestone on Sea
Greatstone on Sea
Lydd on Sea
Dungeness

Stowting
Postling
Stanford
M20
A261
Dymchurch
St. Mary's
Bay

Rye Bay

1
2
3
4
5
6

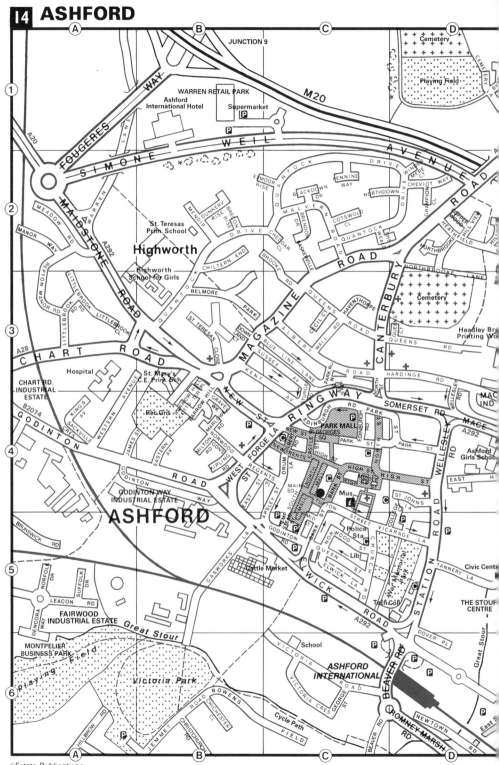

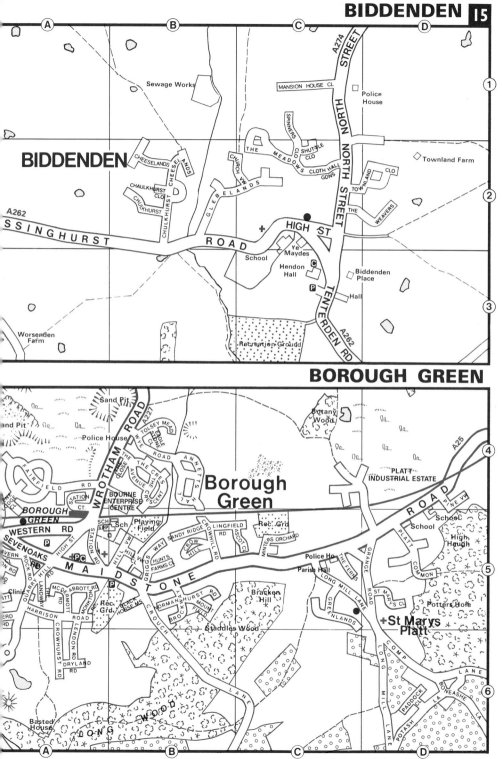

BIDDENDEN

BOROUGH GREEN

Reading Street

Kingsgate College

Convalescent Home

North Foreland Lighthouse

Elmwood Farm

Convalescent Home

Hope Point

Foreland School

Stone Bay School

Recreation Ground

St Peters

BROADSTAIRS

BROADSTAIRS

The Broadway

Library

Upton

Playing Field

Police Sta.

U.D.C. Offices

Viking Bay

Pier

Louisa Bay

RAMSGATE

Technical College

School

School

Playing Field

Dumpton Point

Playing Field

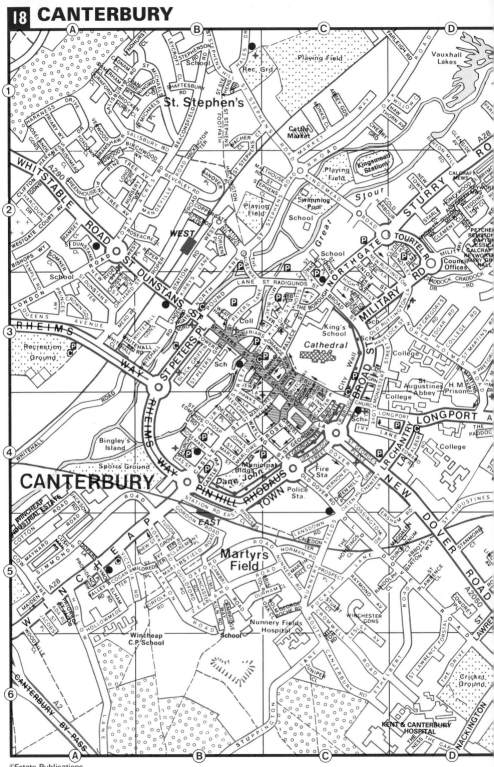

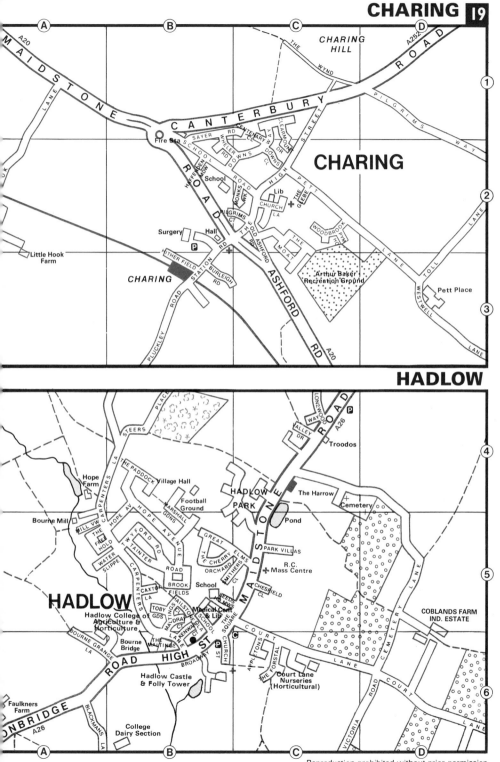

CHARING

HADLOW

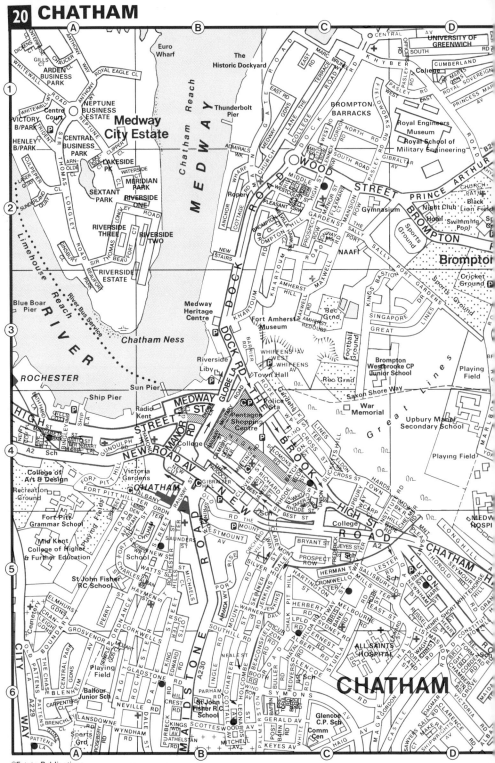

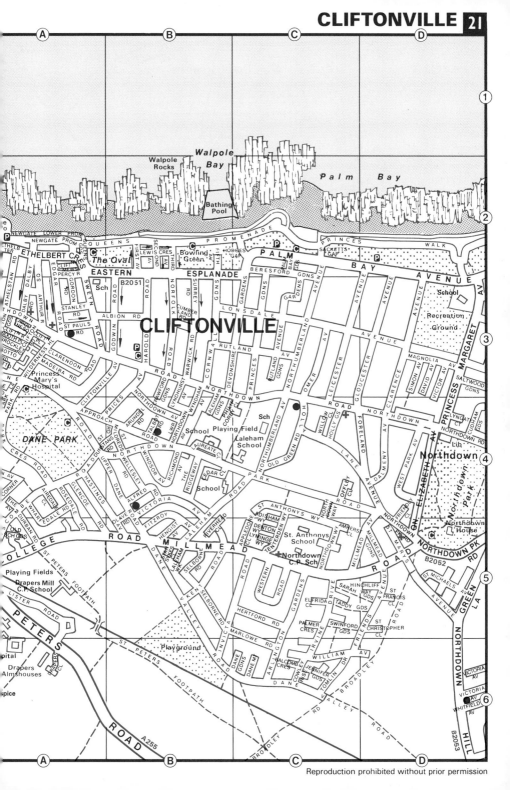

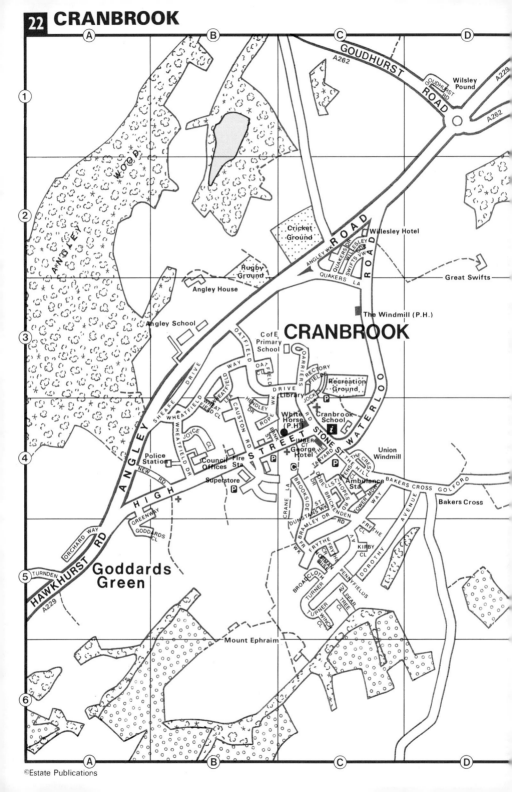

CRANBROOK

GOUDHURST ROAD
GOUDHURST RD
A262
Wilsley Pound
A229
A262

WOOD

ANGLEY

ROAD

Cricket Ground

Willesley Hotel

Rugby Ground

Angley House

Angley WK
QUAKERS DR
WILLESLEY
SWIFTS VW
QUAKERS LA

ROAD

Great Swifts

Angley School

The Windmill (P.H.)

C of E Primary School

OATFIELD WAY
OATFIELD
HEATFIELD DRIVE
SHEAFE DRIVE
WHEATFIELD DRIVE
CAUSTON RD
JOYCE CL
WHEAT FIELD CL
HENDLEY DR
ROPE WK
BANK
CARRIERS FIELDS
RECTORY
DRIVE
Library
JOCK

Recreation Ground

White Horse (P.H.)

Cranbrook School

Police Station

NEW RD

Council Offices
Fire Sta

George Hotel

STONE STREET

WATERLOO ROAD

Union Windmill

Superstore

CRANE LA
BROOKSIDE
ST DUNSTANS WK
BRAMLEY DR
BROADCLOTH WK
FRYTHE
TURNER
TURNER
TURNER
WINCH CL
ST BRICKENDEN RD
HOPES GR
THE HILL
DEFENSE HILL
LOWER WAY
THE CRESS
BAKERS CROSS
AVENUE
DOROTHY
FRYTHE CL
KIRBY CL
PENNYFIELDS
TREE CL
BEAR CL
GOLFORD
Bakers Cross

Ambulance Sta

ANGLEY ROAD

HIGH

HAWKHURST RD
A229
ORCHARD WAY
TURNDEN
GREENWAY
GODDARDS CL

Goddards Green

Mount Ephraim

A B C D
1 2 3 4 5 6

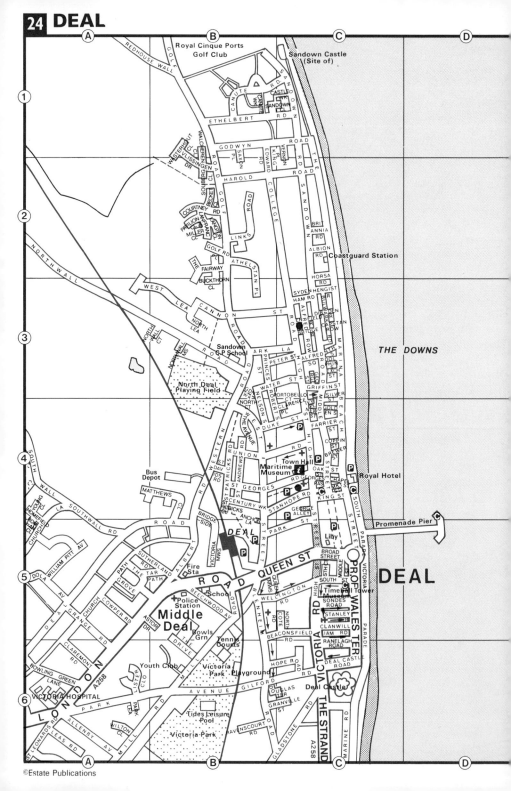

Royal Cinque Ports
Golf Club

Sandown Castle
(Site of)

Coastguard Station

THE DOWNS

Sandown
C.P. School

North Deal
Playing Field

Bus
Depot

Town Hall
Maritime
Museum

Royal Hotel

Promenade Pier

DEAL

Middle
Deal

Fire
Sta

Police
Station

Bowls
Grn

Tennis
Courts

Youth Club

Victoria
Park Playground

Deal Castle

VICTORIA HOSPITAL

Tides Leisure
Pool

Victoria Park

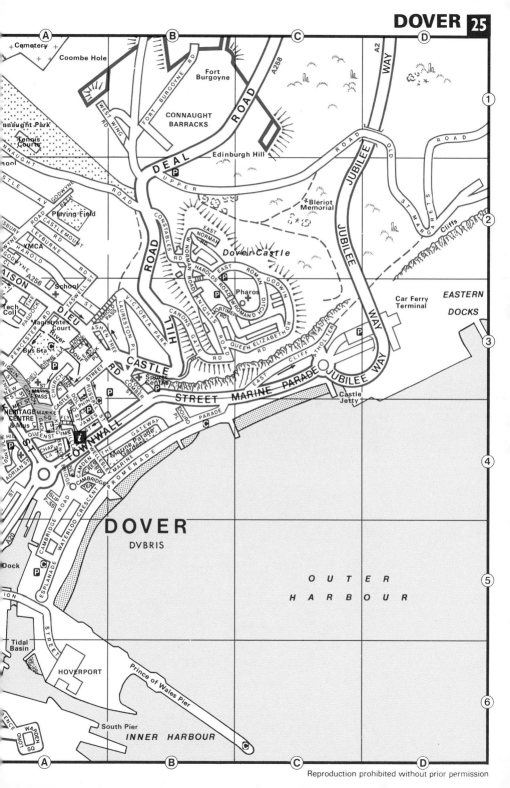

DOVER 25

Cemetery

Coombe Hole

Fort Burgoyne

CONNAUGHT BARRACKS

nnaught Park

Tennis Courts

Playing Field

Edinburgh Hill

Bleriot Memorial

Dover Castle

Pharos

School

YMCA

Magistrates Court

Bus Sta.

Tech Coll

River Dour

MAISON DIEU

Sports Centre

Car Ferry Terminal

EASTERN DOCKS

Castle Jetty

HERITAGE CENTRE & Mus.

Maine Parade Gardens

DOVER

DVBRIS

O U T E R

H A R B O U R

Dock

Tidal Basin

HOVERPORT

Prince of Wales Pier

South Pier

INNER HARBOUR

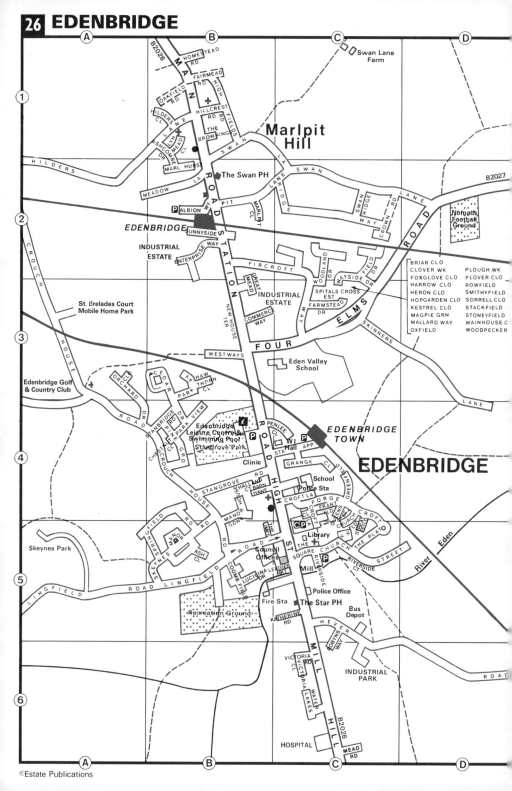

EDENBRIDGE

Marlpit Hill

EDENBRIDGE TOWN

Swan Lane Farm

The Swan PH

Nomads Football Ground

INDUSTRIAL ESTATE

St. Brelades Court Mobile Home Park

INDUSTRIAL ESTATE

Eden Valley School

Edenbridge Golf & Country Club

BRIAR CLO
CLOVER WK
FOXGLOVE CLO
HARROW CLO
HERON CLO
HOPGARDEN CLO
KESTREL CLO
MAGPIE GRN
MALLARD WAY
OXFIELD

PLOUGH WK
PLOVER CLO
ROWFIELD
SMITHYFIELD
SORRELL CLO
STACKFIELD
STONEYFIELD
WAINHOUSE C
WOODPECKER

Edenbridge Leisure Centre & Swimming Pool Stangrove Park

Clinic

School
Police Sta

Library

Council Offices

Mill

Skeynes Park

Police Office
The Star PH
Bus Depot

Fire Sta

Recreation Ground

INDUSTRIAL PARK

HOSPITAL

River Eden

Oare

HAM MARSHES

The Brents

Shipyard

Standing Quay

INDUSTRIAL ESTATE

School

Davington

Community Centre

Primary School

FAVERSHAM

School

Cricket Ground

Town Hall

Police Sta

School

Swim Pool

Health Centre Hosp

EAST ST

Library

Bus Sta

Recreation Ground

Maison Dieu Museum

Playing Field

FAVERSHAM

Ospringe

School

Preston

Playing Field

Fire Sta

Amb Sta

Abbey School

Football Ground

FOLKESTONE

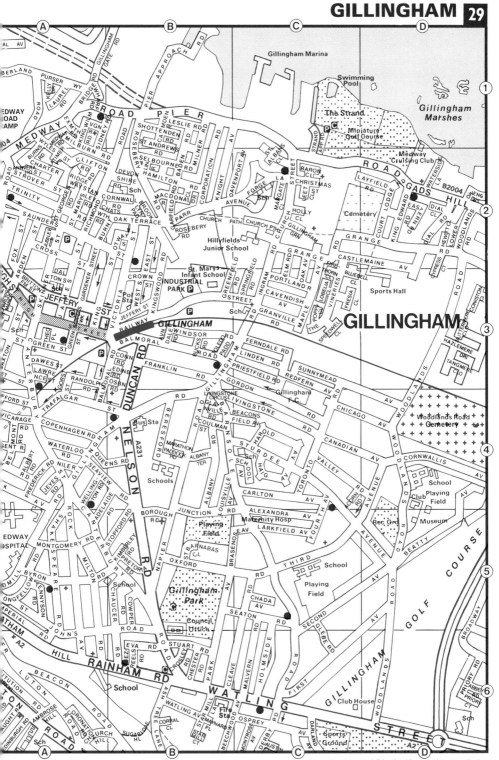

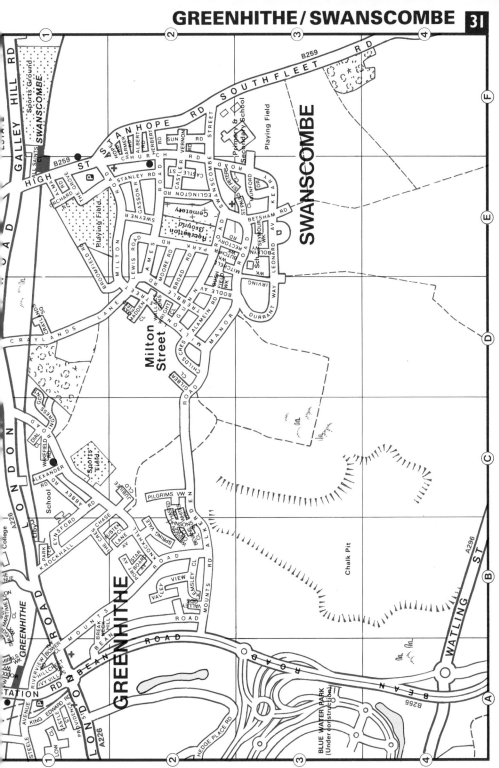

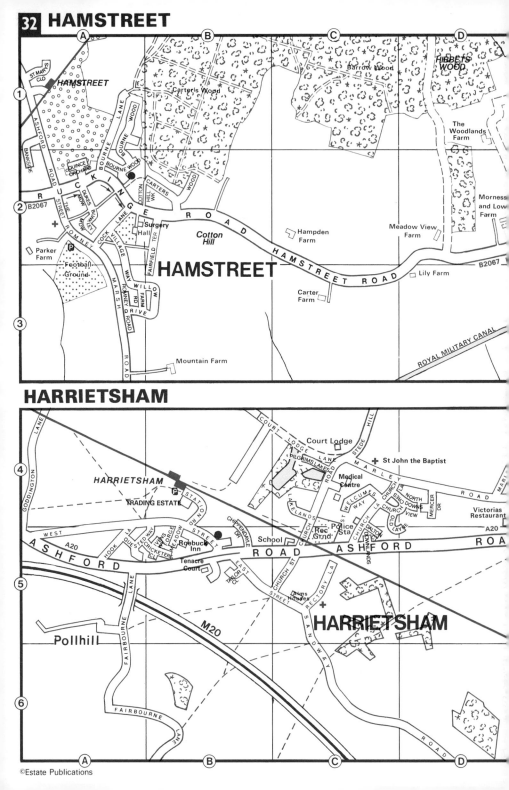

HAMSTREET

HAMSTREET

HARRIETSHAM

HARRIETSHAM

Pollhill

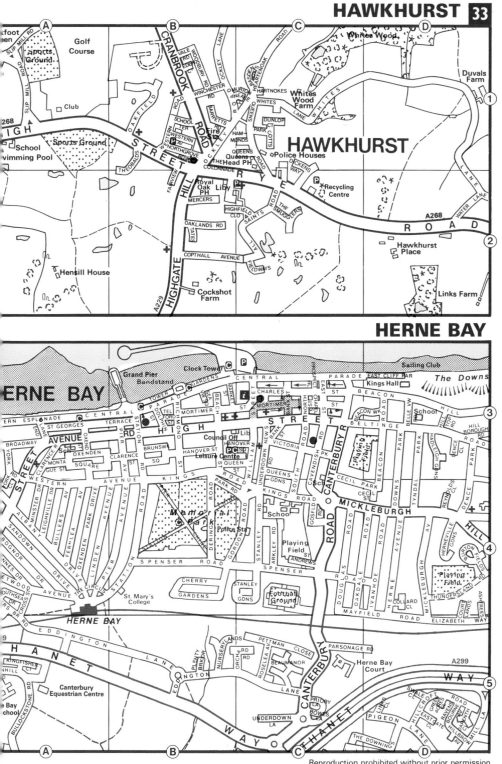

HAWKHURST 33

HERNE BAY

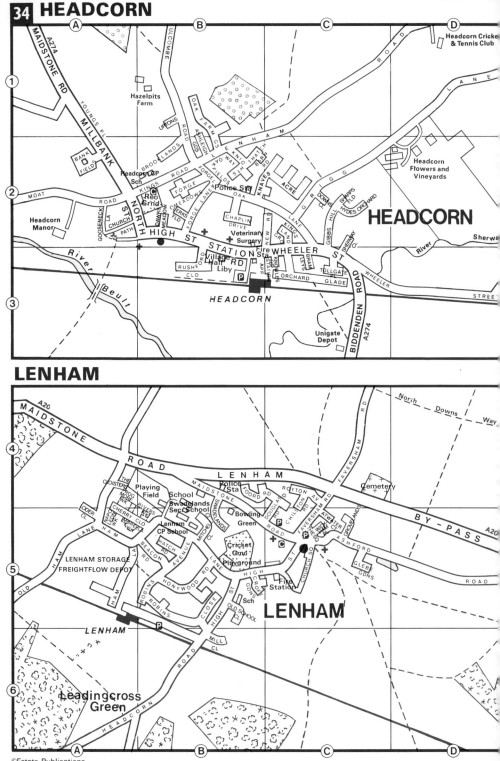

HEADCORN

A274
MAIDSTONE RD
MILLBANK
YOUNGS PL
ULCOMBE

Headcorn Cricket & Tennis Club

Hazelpits Farm

OAK FARM CL
BROOKLANDS
UPTONS
ROAD

ASHLEIGH GDNS
FORGE FIELDS
KNAVES ACRE
LEN HAM
YOLK WAY
HIGH THATCH
BLEN

Headcorn CP Sch
KINGS C
Reo Grid
MOAT
ROAD
GOOSENECK LA
ST NORTH
CHURCH PATH
HIGH
DAWN MEADOW
CLERKS FLD
FORGE MEADOW
FORGE LANE RD
OAK
CHAPLIN DRIVE
Police Sta
Veterinary Surgery
NEW RD
LINKS LAND CR
LINKS
BRAM LEYS
KNOT FIELDS

Headcorn Flowers and Vineyards

Headcorn Manor

River Beult

STATION RD
Village Hall
Liby
RUSH CLO
 + Fire Sta
WHEELER ST
APP
ORCHARD
TOLLGATE GLADE
SHENLEY CL
GIBBS HILL
DOWNS
HYDES ORCHARD

HEADCORN

River
Sherw

WHEELER ROAD
STREE

HEADCORN

BIDDENDEN ROAD
A274

Unigate Depot

A20
MAIDSTONE
ROAD

North Downs Way

LENHAM

FAVERSHAM RD
Cemetery
BY - PASS
A20

CROISTERS
THE FROG MEAD
MEAD WY
Playing Field
RIVERS
NAPLETON
CHERRY CLO
MOW RY
CL DER CL
School
Swadelands Sec School
Lenham CP School
Police Sta
MAIDSTONE
FOORD RD
ROYTON AV
CHILLTON RD
DOUGLAS RD
ATWATER
GROVELANDS
ASHFORD
ROAD
GLEBE GDNS
ROAD

LENHAM STORAGE FREIGHTFLOW DEPOT

HAM LANE
BEACON RD
HATCH
AVENUE
MITCH
SWADELANDS
LANE
Bowling Green
Cricket Grnd
Playground
HONYWOOD RD
CLOSE
ROBINS
ROBINS
HIGH ST
CROFT GDNS
OLD SCHOOL CL
HIGH ST
Fire Station
Sch
CHURCH SQ

LENHAM

OLD
LA
HAM
LENHAM
MILL CL
ROAD

Leadingcross Green

HEADCORN LANE

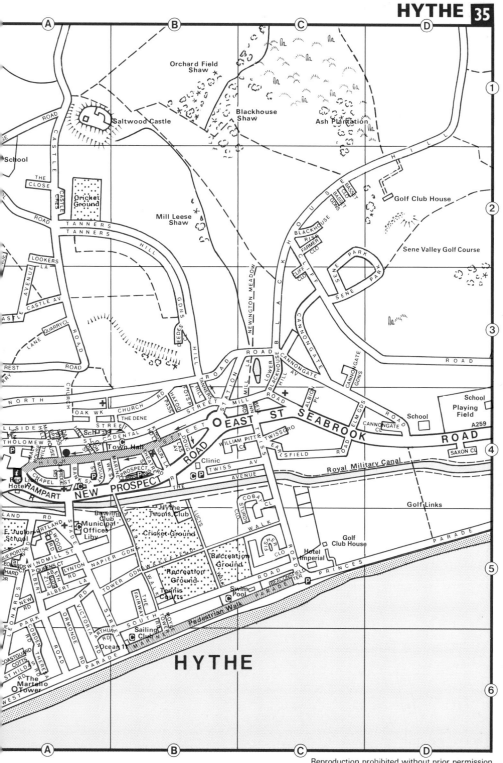

HYTHE

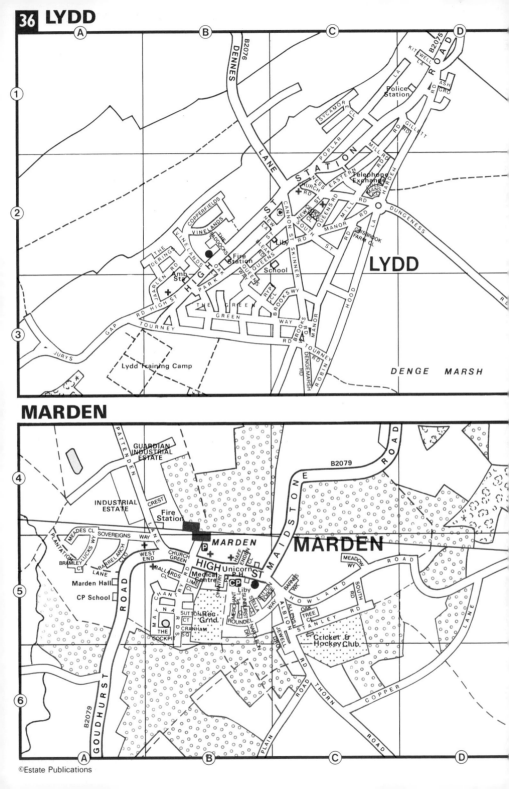

MARDEN

DENGE MARSH

LYDD

MARDEN

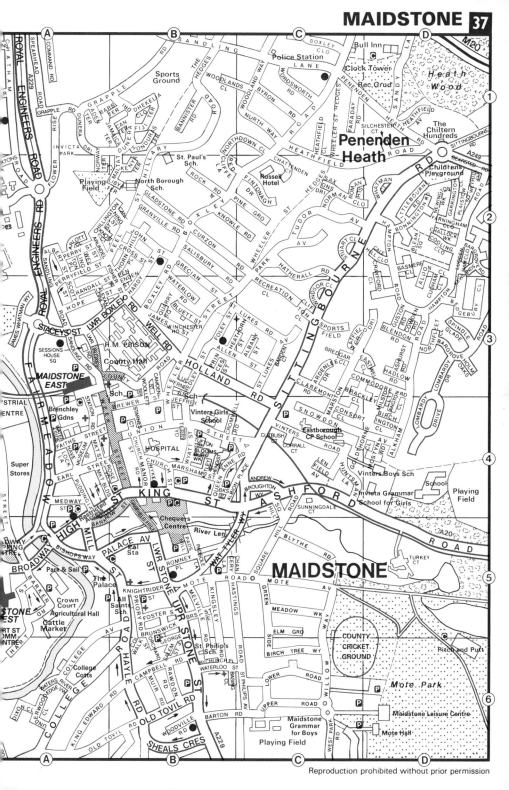

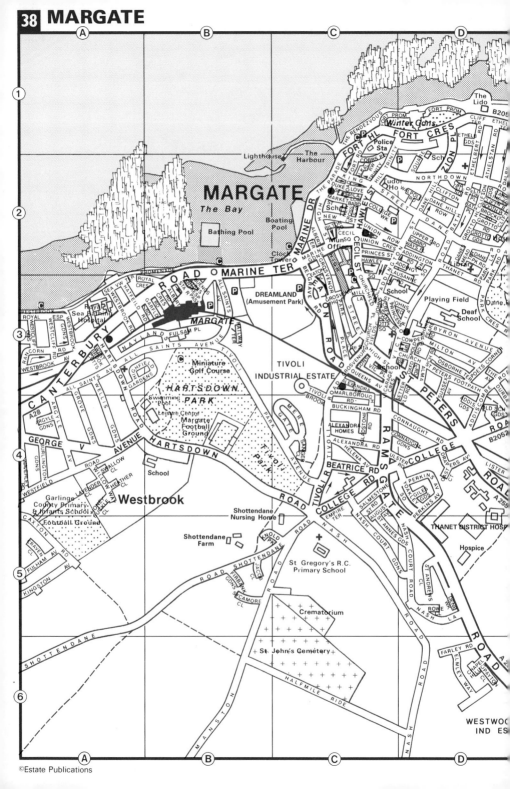

MARGATE
The Bay

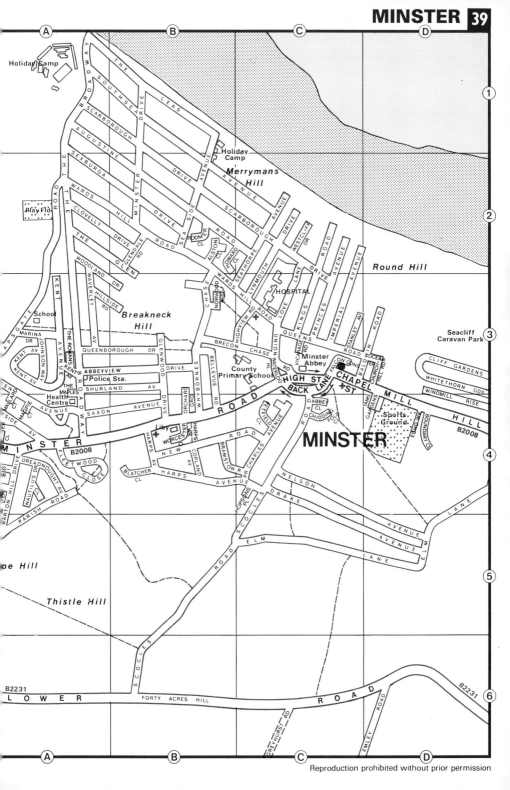

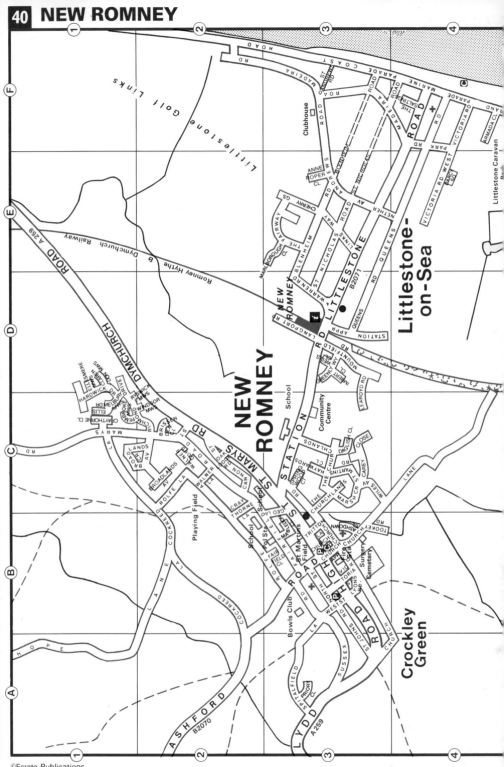

NEW ROMNEY

Littlestone-on-Sea

Crockley Green

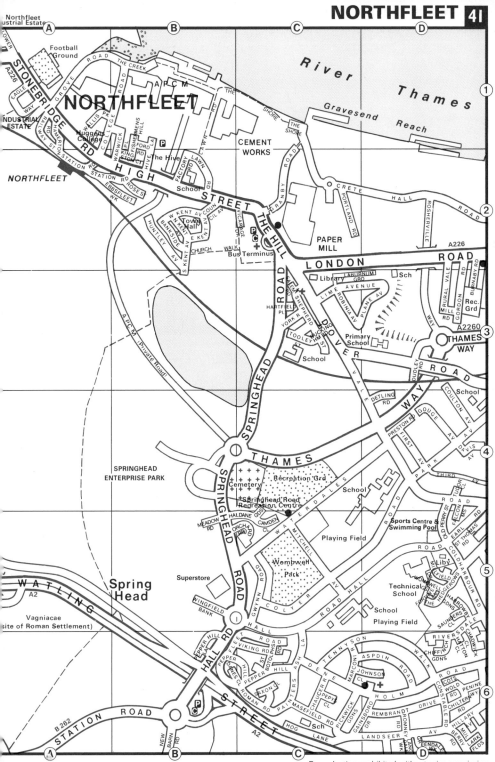

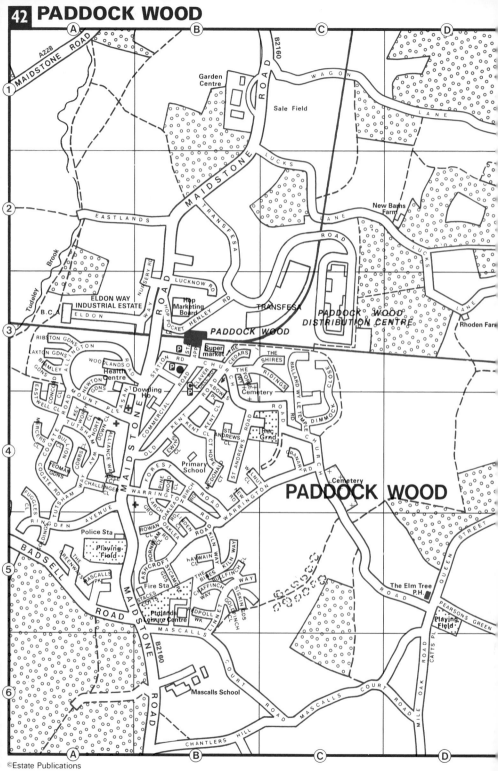

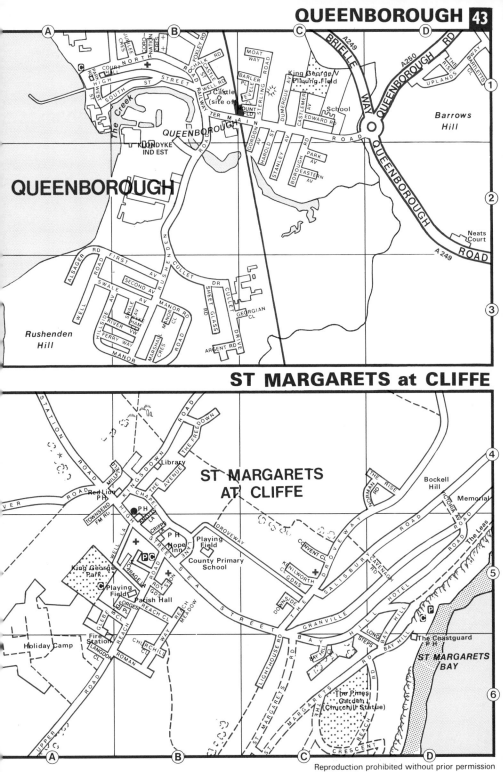

QUEENBOROUGH

ST MARGARETS at CLIFFE

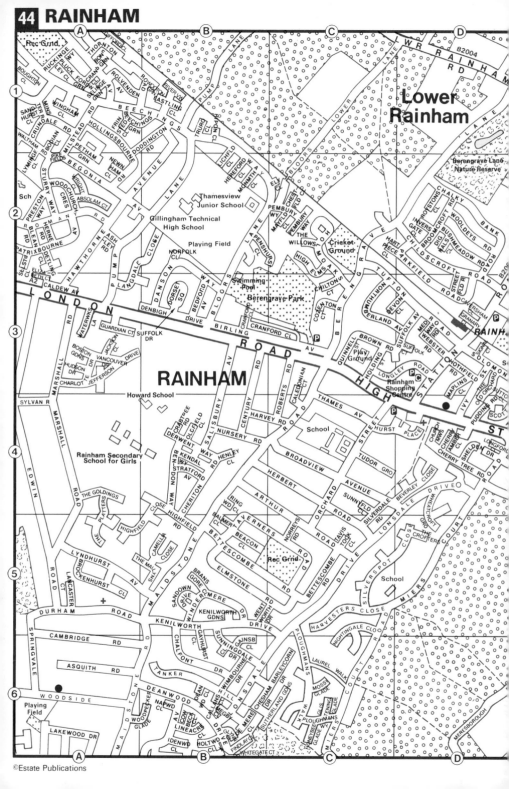

44 RAINHAM

Lower Rainham

RAINHAM

RAMSGATE

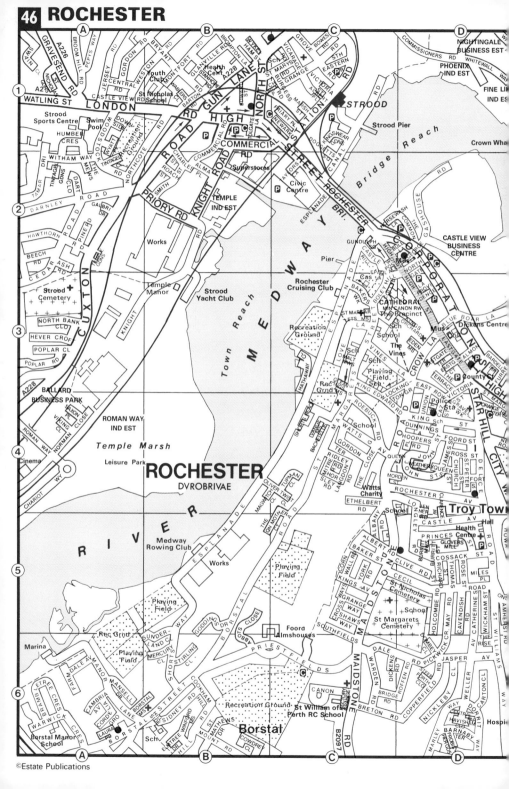

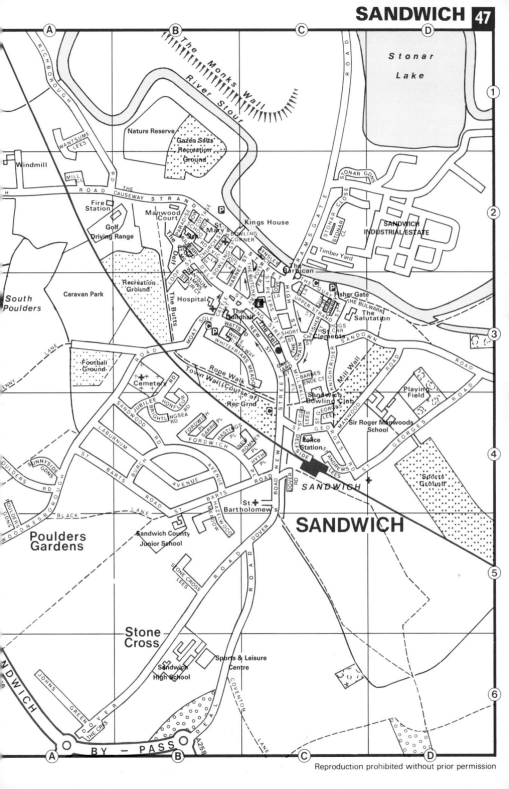

A   B   C   D

Stonar Lake

Nature Reserve
Gazen Salts Recreation Ground

The Monks Wall
River Stour

Windmill

Fire Station
Manwood Court
Golf Driving Range

St Mary's
Kings House
Bowling Corner

SANDWICH INDUSTRIAL ESTATE

Timber Yard
The Barbican

South Poulders
Caravan Park
Recreation Ground
Hospital
The Butts

Fisher Gate
The Bulwark
The Salutation
The Guildhall
St Clements

Football Ground
Cemetery
Rope Walk
Town Wall (Course of)
Rec Grnd

Sandwich Bowling Club
Playing Field
Sir Roger Manwoods School
Mill Wall

Poulders Gardens
Sandwich County Junior School

St Bartholomew's
Police Station
SANDWICH

Sports Ground

Stone Cross
Sandwich High School
Sports & Leisure Centre

A   BY - PASS   B   A258   C   D

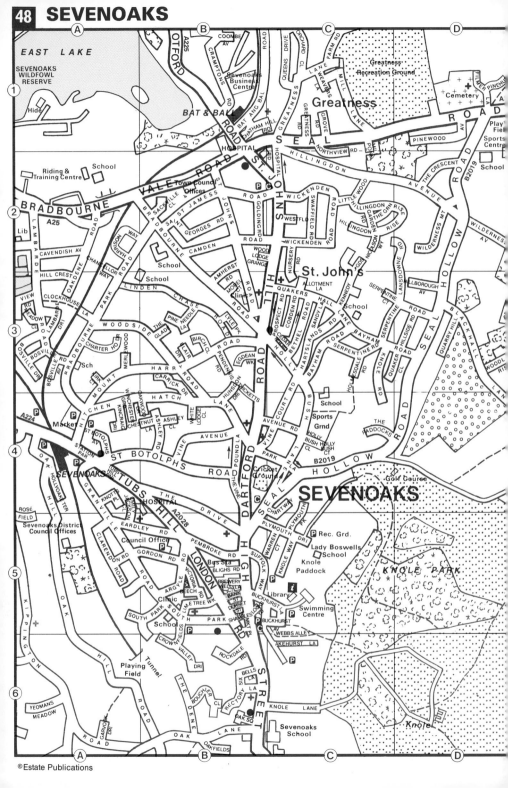

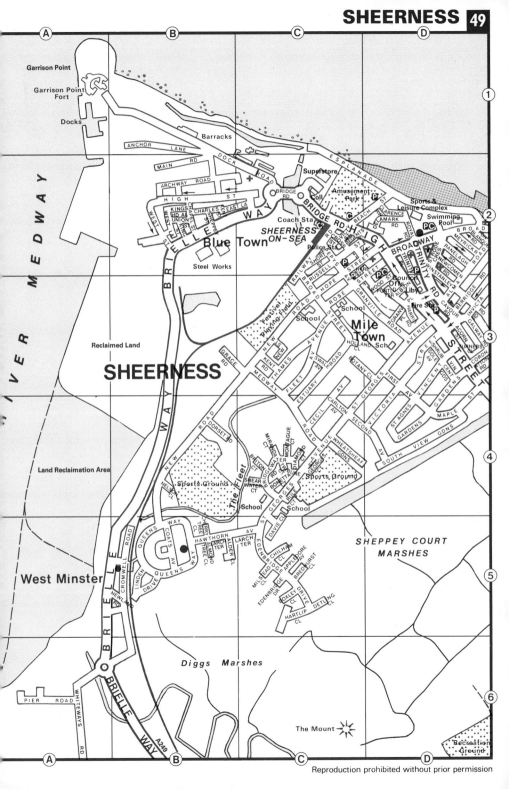

Garrison Point

Garrison Point Fort

Docks

Barracks

ANCHOR LANE

MAIN RD

ARCHWAY ROAD

HIGH ST

WEST KINGS RD

CHARLES ST

SHEPPEY ST

EAST LA

UNION ST

BRIDGE RD

Coll

Coach Sta

SHEERNESS ON-SEA

Blue Town

Steel Works

ESPLANADE

Superstore

Amusement Park

Sports & Leisure Complex

Swimming Pool

CLARENCE RD

BEACH ST

ROYAL RD

Police Sta

BRIDGE RD

HIGH STREET

BROADWAY

TRINITY RD

BROAD

BLAND

MEYRICK RD

RANELAGH

NEW ORLEANS RD

STANLEY RD

BEBRIDGE RD

HARRIS

CAZOR

INVICTA

GALWAY RD

CORON RD

RAILWAY ST

SHORT ST

RUSSELL

HOPE ST

ROSE ST

School

GRANVILLE ROAD

WOOD ST

PC

Council Offe

Lby

Fire Sta

HIGH ST

MILE Town

HOLLAND Sch

CECIL AV

ST AGNES AV

VINCENT AV

VICTORIA

SECOND AV

GEORGE

FIRST AV

SWALE ROAD

ESTUARY

FLEET

MEDWAY

THAMES

NEW ROAD

KENT RD

AVENUE

AVENUE

NEW RD

GRACE RD

Reclaimed Land

SHEERNESS

Festival Playing Field

School

BOTANY CL

TURNERS

ACORN

SHRUB

CTS

COSTS

MAPLE

GARDENS

SOUTH VIEW GDNS

STREET

DORSET RD

MONTAGUE

MIRANDA CT

BRIDGEWATER

BONETTS

DIAMOND

GEORGES CT

PRUNE

CARLTON AV

WHEATSHEAF GDNS

ROAD

Sports Ground

AVENUE

Land Reclaimation Area

The Fleet

Sports Ground

SHEAR WATER CT

School

ST GEORGES RD

School

NELSON CL

WAY

QUEENS ROAD

COATS AV

HAWTHORN AV

HERB TREE CL

ADDER CL

LARCH TER

ARCH TER

DAVIE CL

EDENBRIDGE DR

MILSTEAD CHILHAM CL

APPLEDORE

BREDHURST CL

DETLING CL

HARTLIP CL

FOXLEY DRIVE

EDENBRIDGE

QUEENS DRIVE

LINDEN

NEWLAND

CROMWELL ROAD

West Minster

BRIELLE WAY

B R I E L L E   W A Y

SHEPPEY COURT MARSHES

Diggs Marshes

PIER ROAD

WHITEWAYS RD

A249

The Mount

Recreation Ground

R I V E R   M E D W A Y

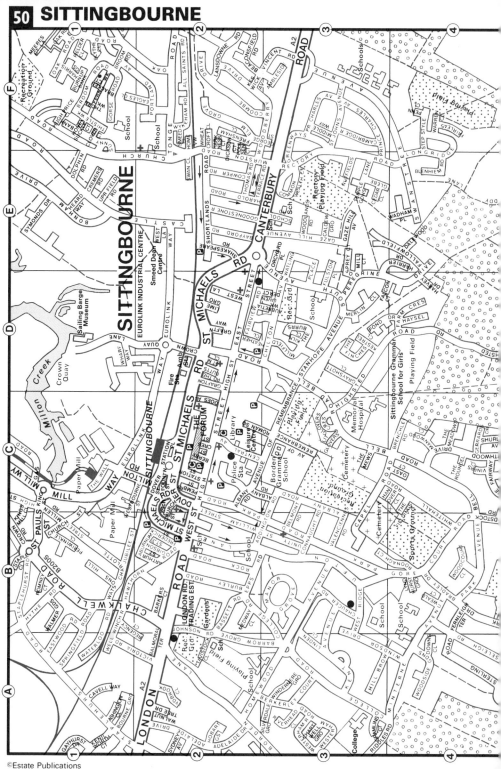

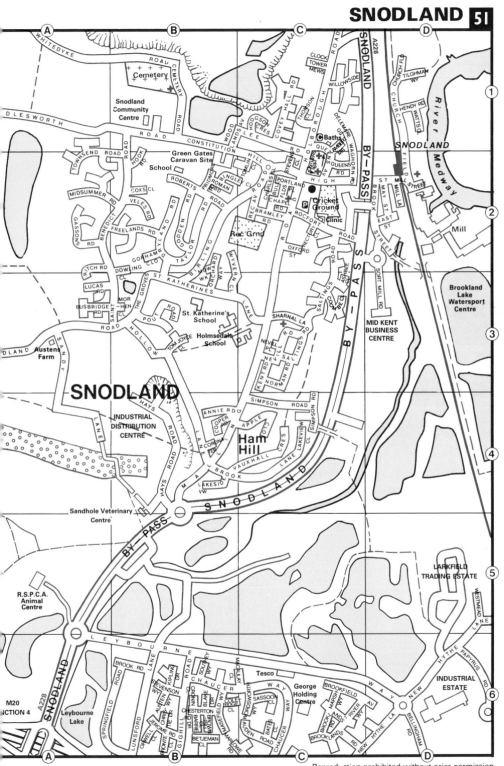

SNODLAND 51

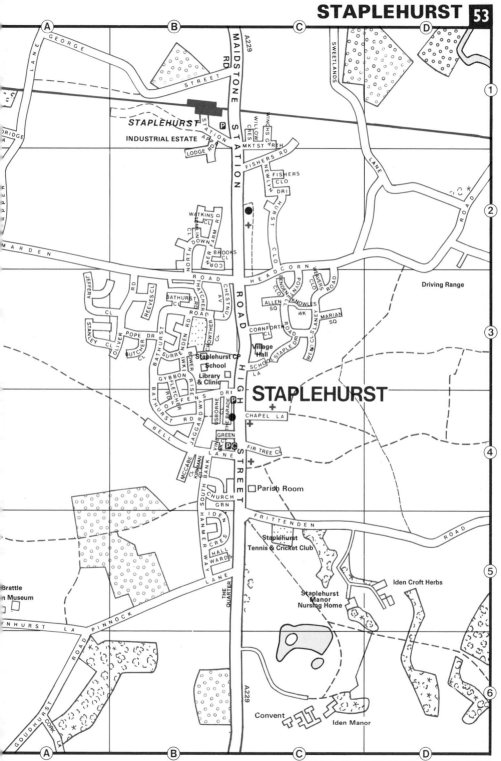

STAPLEHURST

STAPLEHURST
INDUSTRIAL ESTATE

Village
Hall

Staplehurst CP
School

Library
& Clinic

Driving Range

CHAPEL LA

Parish Room

Staplehurst
Tennis & Cricket Club

Iden Croft Herbs

Brattle
n Museum

Staplehurst
Manor
Nursing Home

Convent

Iden Manor

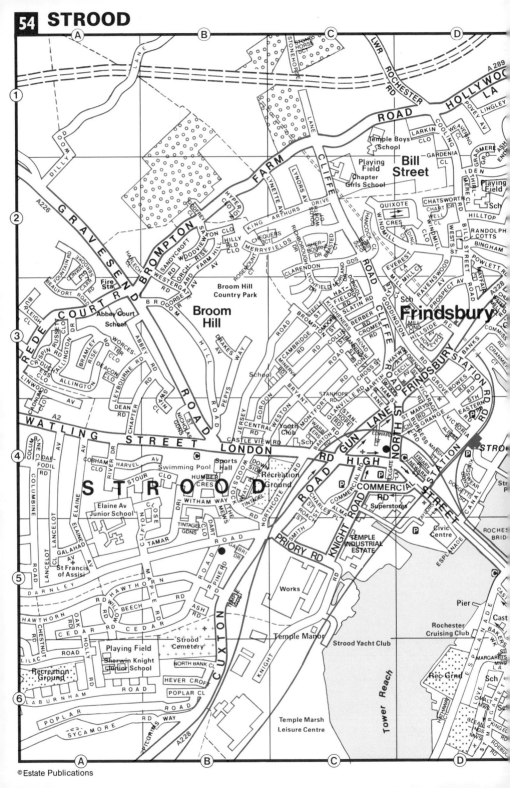

54 STROOD

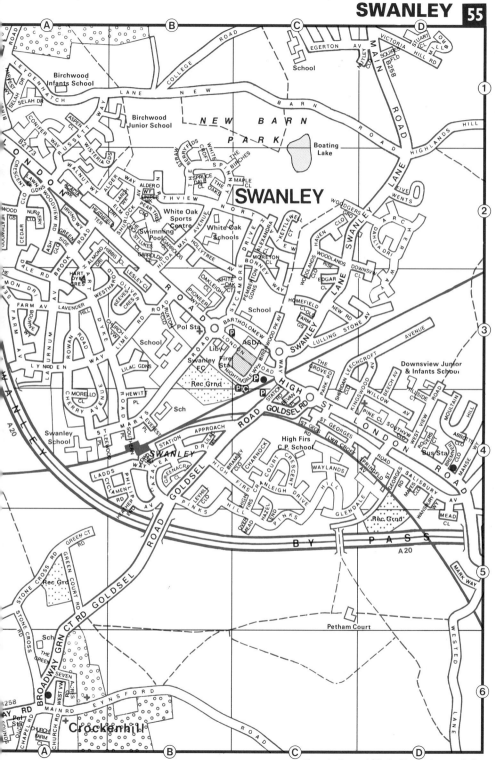

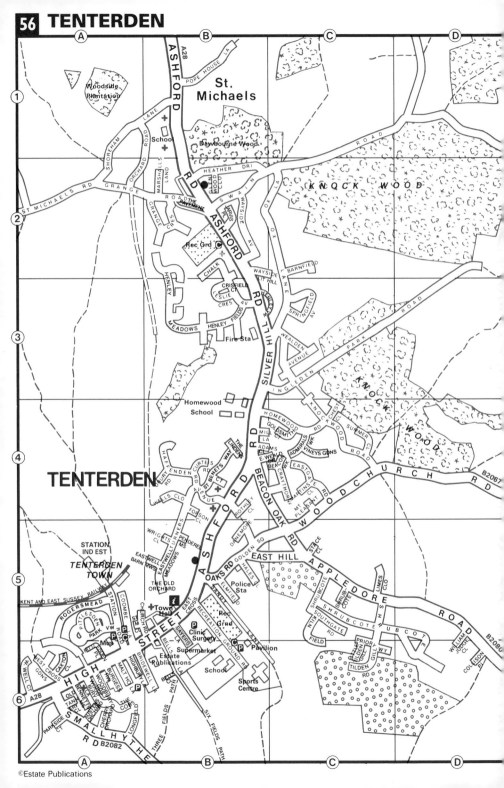

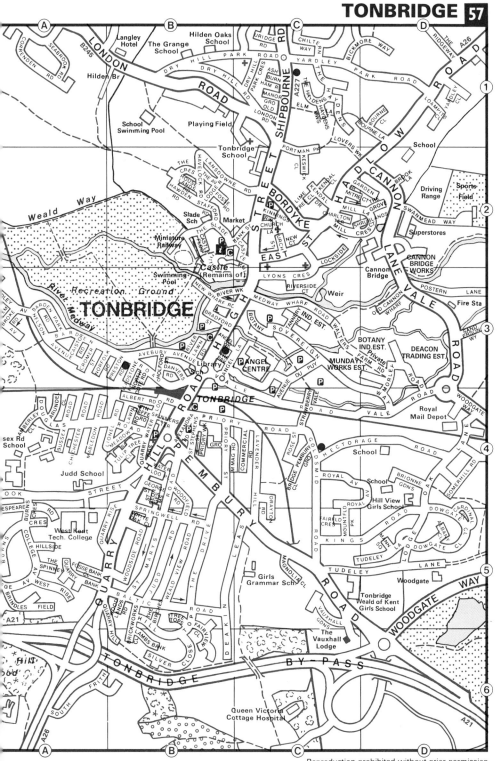

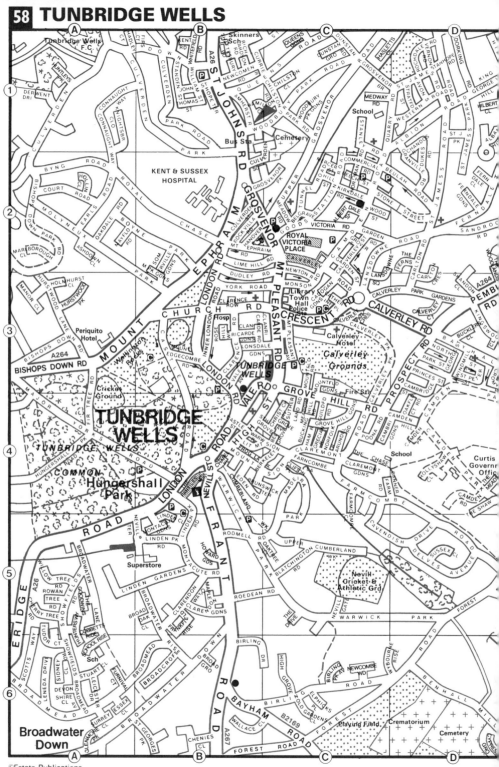

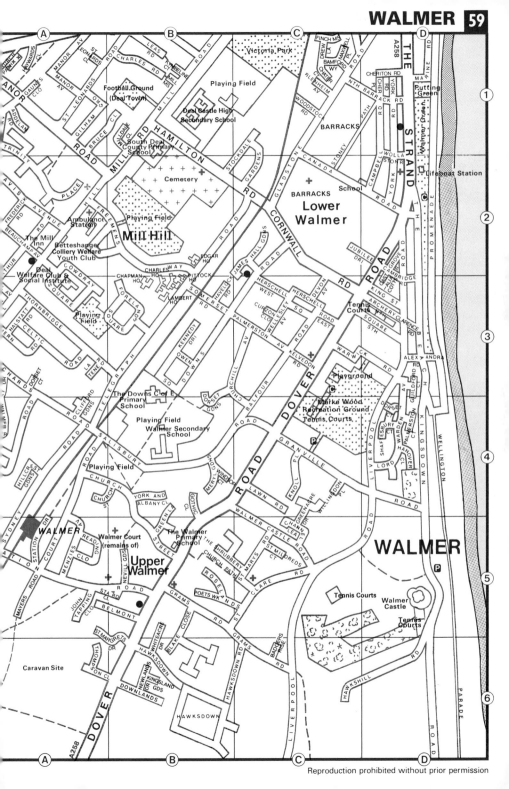

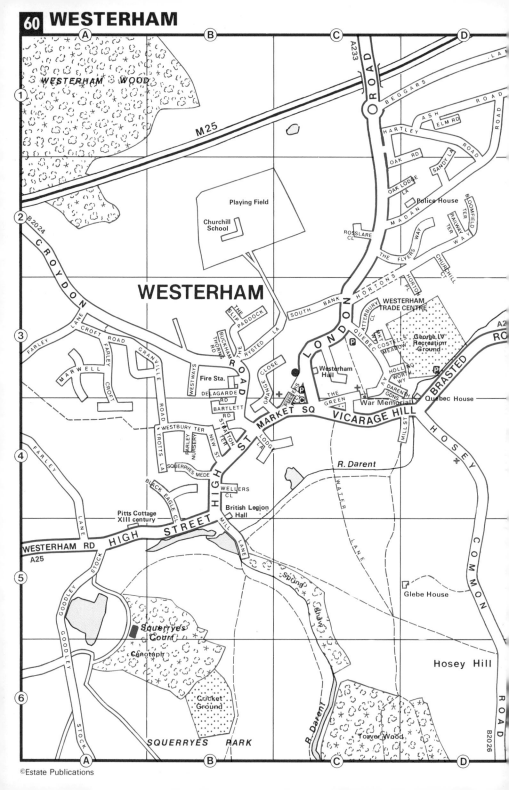

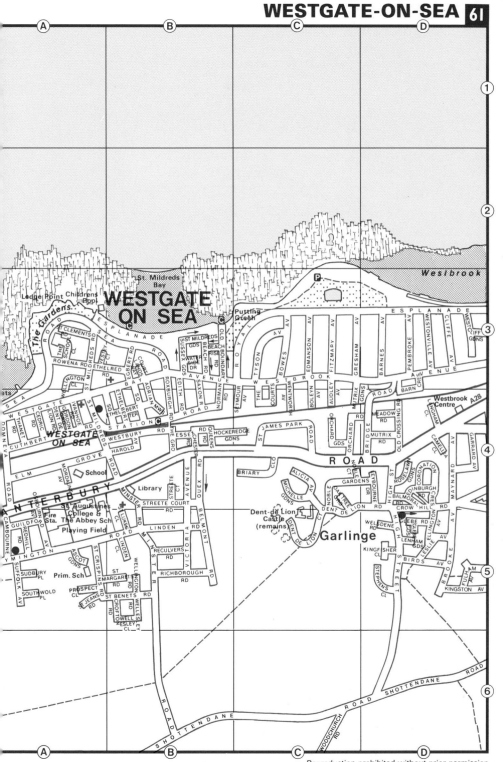

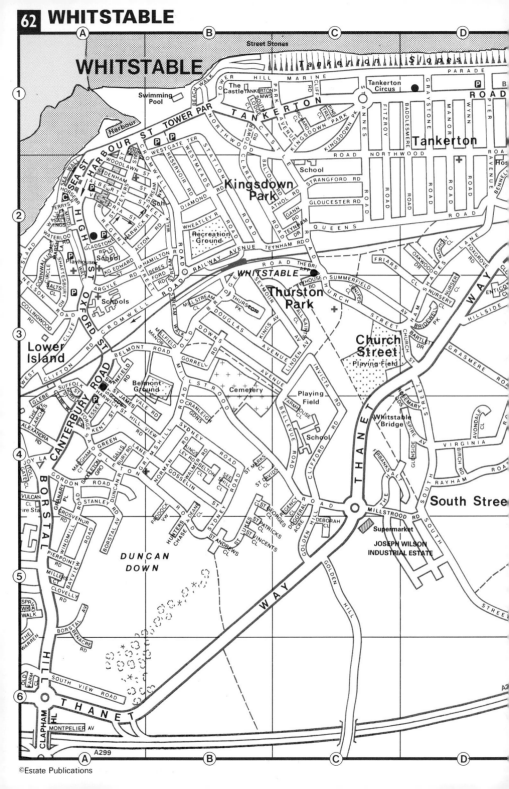

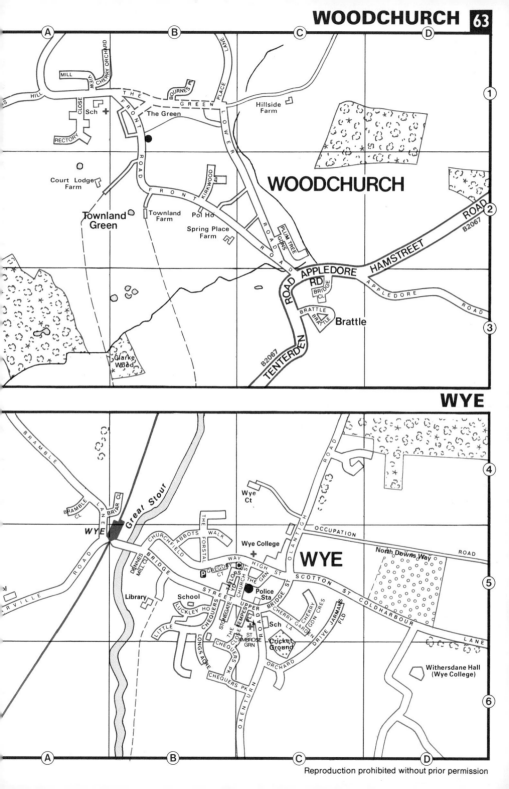

WYE

The Index includes some names for which there is insufficient space on the maps. These names are preceded by an * and are followed by the nearest adjoining thoroughfare.

ollingwood Clo. CT10 17 A5
onvent Rd. CT10 17 B1
ornwallis Gdns. CT10 17 C3
oronation Clo. CT10 17 A1
rawford Rd. CT10 17 B4
rescent Rd. CT10 17 D1
rofts Pl. CT10 17 C4
row Hill. CT10 17 C3
umberland Av. CT10 17 C3
almaney Clo. CT10 17 C3
arnley Clo. CT10 17 A6
avids Clo. CT10 17 C6
evonshire Ter. CT10 17 C4
ckens Rd. CT10 17 D4
orcas Gdns. CT10 17 B2
ouglas Clo. CT10 17 A3
umpton Pk Dri. CT10 17 C6
undonald Rd. CT10 17 C5
ast Cliff Prom. CT10 17 D3
astern Esplanade. CT10 17 D3
dge End Rd. CT10 17 B5
izabeth Ct. CT10 17 D2
mwood Av. CT10 17 C1
mwood Clo. CT10 17 B1
thel Rd. CT10 17 B4
air St. CT10 17 A5
airacre. CT10 17 A5
airfield Park. CT10 17 A4
airfield Rd. CT10 17 A4
ern Ct. CT10 17 D4
ig Tree Rd. CT10 17 B2
ordoun Rd. CT10 17 B4
ordwich Gro. CT10 17 A2
ort Rd. CT10 17 D4
osters Av. CT10 17 A2
rancis Rd. CT10 17 C2
ladstone Rd. CT10 17 B5
loucester Av. CT10 17 A5
rafton Rd. CT10 17 A1
range Rd. CT10 17 A2
range Way. CT10 17 B6
rant Clo. CT10 17 A3
ranville Av. CT10 17 C5
ranville Rd. CT10 17 C5
reen La. CT10 17 A4
renville Way. CT10 17 A5
rosvenor Rd. CT10 17 B5
uy Clo. CT10 17 C2
arbour St. CT10 17 D4
armsworth Gdns. CT10 17 B3
arrow Dene. CT10 17 A3
igh St, Broadstairs. CT10 17 C4
igh St, St Peter's. CT10 17 A3
ildersham Clo. CT10 17 A3
iller Clo. CT10 17 B3
olm Oak Gdns. CT10 17 B5
oward Rd. CT10 17 C5
ubert Way. CT10 17 A2
ugin Av. CT10 17 A1
nverness Ter. CT10 17 C5
ohn St. CT10 17 D5
ulie Clo. CT10 17 B2
endal Rise. CT10 17 B3
ing Edwards Av. CT10 17 C5
ingfisher Walk. CT10 17 A4
ings Av. CT10 17 C3
nights Av. CT10 17 C3
aking Av. CT10 17 C2
anthorne Rd. CT10 17 B2
auriston Mount. CT10 17 B3
awn Rd. CT10 17 C4
eatt Clo. CT10 17 A5
erryn Gdns. CT10 17 B1
eybourn Rd. CT10 17 C6
inden Av. CT10 17 C3
indenthorpe Rd. CT10 17 B3
ink Rd. CT10 17 A1
inley Rd. CT10 17 A2
ivingstone Rd. CT10 17 A3
loyd Rd. CT10 17 B4
uton Av. CT10 17 B5
uton Ct. CT10 17 B5
yndhurst Rd. CT10 17 C3
Magdala Rd. CT10 17 A3
Magdelen Ct. CT10 17 C3
Manor Rd. CT10 17 B5
Marlborough Clo. CT10 17 A6
Marshall Cres. CT10 17 A5
Masons Rise. CT10 17 B4
Maxine Gdns. CT10 17 A3
Mayville Rd. CT10 17 A2
Millfield. CT10 17 B3
Mockett Dri. CT10 17 A1
Napier Rd. CT10 17 A3
Nash Gdns. CT10 17 C4
Nelson Pl. CT10 17 D4
Norman Rd. CT10 17 A3
North Foreland Av. CT10 17 D2
North Foreland Rd. CT10 17 D2
Northcliffe Gdns. CT10 17 B2
Northdown Rd. CT10 17 A2
Old Green Rd. CT10 17 B2
Old Kingsdown Clo. CT10 17 A6
Osborne Rd. CT10 17 B5
Oscar Rd. CT10 17 C5
Palmerston Av. CT10 17 C6
Park Av. CT10 17 A6
Park Chase. CT10 17 A6
Park Gate. CT10 17 A6
Park Rd. CT10 17 D3
Parkland Ct. CT10 17 B3
Percy Rd. CT10 17 B4
Pier App. CT10 17 D4
Pierremont Av. CT10 17 C4
Poplar Rd. CT10 17 A3
Prince Andrew Rd. CT10 17 A2
Prince Charles Rd. CT10 17 A1
Princess Anne Rd. CT10 17 A2
Priory Clo. CT10 17 B6
Promenade. CT10 17 D5
Prospect Pl. CT10 17 C4
Prospect Rd. CT10 17 C4
Queens Av. CT10 17 C3
Queens Gdns. CT10 17 C5
Queens Rd. CT10 17 C5
Radley Clo. CT10 17 C3
Raglan Pl. CT10 17 C5
Ramsgate Rd. CT10 17 B6
Ranelagh Gro. CT10 17 A4
Reading St. CT10 17 B1
Reading Street Rd. CT10 17 A1
Rectory Rd. CT10 17 D4
Repton Clo. CT10 17 A3
Rhodes Gdns. CT10 17 B2
Rosemary Av. CT10 17 B6
Rosemary Gdns. CT10 17 B6
Rosetower Ct. CT10 17 B1
Royal Clo. CT10 17 A5
Rugby Clo. CT10 17 A3
St Christophers Grn. CT10 17 B4
St Georges Rd. CT10 17 C5
St James Av. CT10 17 A4
St Marys Rd. CT10 17 C4
St Mildreds Av. CT10 17 B5
St Peters Ct. CT10 17 B3
St Peters Pk Rd. CT10 17 B3
St Peters Rd. CT10 17 A4
Salisbury Av. CT10 17 B6
Salts Dri. CT10 17 A4
Sanctuary Clo. CT10 17 B6
Sea App. CT10 17 D5
Sea View Rd. CT10 17 C3
Seafield Rd. CT10 17 B5
Seapoint Rd. CT10 17 C6
Selwyn Dri. CT10 17 A4
Shutler Rd. CT10 17 D4
Sowell St. CT10 17 B4
Speke Rd. CT10 17 A3
Staines Pl. CT10 17 C4
Stanley Pl. CT10 17 C4
Stanley Rd. CT10 17 B3
Stephen Clo. CT10 17 C5
Sterling Clo. CT10 17 A3
Stone Gdns. CT10 17 C4
Stone Rd. CT10 17 D4
Swinburne Av. CT10 17 B5
Thanet Clo. CT10 17 C4
Thanet Place Gdns. CT10 17 D2
Thanet Rd. CT10 17 C4
The Banks. CT10 17 B3
The Broadway. CT10 17 B4
The Oaks. CT10 17 B2
The Paddocks. CT10 17 B2
The Parade. CT10 17 D5
The Pathway. CT10 17 C4
The Promenade. CT10 17 D5
The Ridgeway. CT10 17 A6
The Vale. CT10 17 B5
Tina Gdns. CT10 17 C3
Tippledore La. CT10 17 A3
Trinity Sq. CT10 17 B1
Tunis Row. CT10 17 C4
Union Sq. CT10 17 D4
Upper Approach Rd. CT10 17 C5
Upton Rd. CT10 17 B4
Vale Rd. CT10 17 A5
Vere Rd. CT10 17 C4
Victoria Par. CT10 17 C5
Victoria Rd. CT10 17 A3
Viking Ct. CT10 17 C6
Vine Clo. CT10 17 A6
Waldron Rd. CT10 17 C6
Wallace Way. CT10 17 A5
Walmsley Rd. CT10 17 B4
Wardour Clo. CT10 17 C4
Warren Dri. CT10 17 A4
Wayne Clo. CT10 17 A3
Wellesley Clo. CT10 17 A6
West Cliff Av. CT10 17 C5
West Cliff Prom. CT10 17 D6
West Cliff Rd. CT10 17 C5
Western Esplanade. CT10 17 D6
Westover Gdns. CT10 17 A2
Westover Rd. CT10 17 A2
Whitfield Av. CT10 17 A1
Wilkes Rd. CT10 17 A5
Wings Clo. CT10 17 D3
Wrotham Av. CT10 17 C5
Wrotham Rd. CT10 17 C5
Yarrow Clo. CT10 17 C5
York Av. CT10 17 C5
York St. CT10 17 C5

CANTERBURY

Abbey Gdns. CT2 18 C1
Abbots Barton Wk. CT1 18 D5
Abbots Pl. CT1 18 C3
Ada Rd. CT1 18 A5
Adelaide Pl. CT1 18 B4
Albert Rd. CT1 18 D4
Albion Pl. CT1 18 C3
Alma Pl. CT1 18 D2
Alma St. CT1 18 D2
Ann Green Wk. CT1 18 D2
Artillery Gdns. CT1 18 C3
Artillery St. CT1 18 C3
Barton Mill Rd. CT1 18 D1
Beaconsfield Rd. CT2 18 B1
Beer Cart La. CT1 18 B4
Best La. CT1 18 B3
Beverley Rd. CT2 18 B2
Birchwood Wk. CT2 18 A1
Bishops Way. CT2 18 A2
Black Griffin La. CT1 18 B3
Blackfriars St. CT1 18 C3
Bramshaw Rd. CT2 18 A2
Bristol Rd. CT1 18 C5
Broad Oak Rd. CT2 18 C2
Broad St. CT1 18 C3
Brockenhurst Clo. CT2 18 A1
Brymore Clo. CT1 18 D2
Brymore Rd. CT1 18 D2
Burgate. CT1 18 C3
Burgate La. CT1 18 C4
Butchery La. CT1 18 C3
Cadnam Clo. CT2 18 A1
Calcraft Mewsv 18 D2
Caledon Ter. CT1 18 C5
Cambridge Rd. CT1 18 B5
Cambridge Way. CT1 18 B5
Canterbury By-Pass. CT1 18 A6
Canterbury La. CT1 18 C4
Castle St. CT1 18 B4
Castle Vw. CT1 18 B4
Cherry Gro. CT2 18 C1
Church La. CT1 18 B4
Church St. CT2 18 A3
Church St. CT1 18 C4
Claremont Pl. CT1 18 B5
Clement Clo. CT1 18 D2
Clifton Gdns. CT2 18 A2
Clyde St. CT1 18 D2
Cogan Ter. CT1 18 A5
Cold Harbour. CT1 18 C2
College Rd. CT1 18 D3
Coopers La. CT1 18 A5
Coppergate. CT2 18 B2
Cossington Rd. CT1 18 C5
Cotton Rd. CT1 18 A5
Cow La. CT1 18 A5
Cowdrey Pl. CT1 18 D5
Craddock Dri. CT1 18 D3
Craddock Rd. CT1 18 D3
Cranborne Wk. CT2 18 A1
Cromwell Rd. CT1 18 C5
Cross St. CT2 18 A3
Crown Gdns. CT2 18 A3
Cushman Rd. CT1 18 A5
Damerham Clo. CT2 18 A1
Dover St. CT1 18 C4
Duck La. CT1 18 C3
Durham Clo. CT1 18 B5
Durnford Clo. CT2 18 A1
Durovernum Ct. CT1 18 D5
Edgar Rd. CT1 18 D3
Edward Rd. CT1 18 D4
Elham Rd. CT1 18 A5
Ersham Rd. CT1 18 C5
Ethelbert Rd. CT1 18 C6
Farleigh Rd. CT2 18 D1
Forty Acres Rd. CT2 18 A2
Foxdown Clo. CT2 18 A1
Friary Way. CT2 18 A1
Gas St. CT1 18 B4
George Roche Rd. CT1 18 C5
Gillon Mews. CT1 18 D2
Glenside Av. CT1 18 D1
Gordon Rd. CT1 18 B5
Gravel Wk. CT1 18 C4
Greenhouse La. CT2 18 A2
Grove Ter. CT1 18 B5
Guildford Rd. CT1 18 B5
Guildhall St. CT1 18 C3
Hackington Pl. CT2 18 B2
Hackington Ter. CT2 18 B1
Hales Dri. CT2 18 B1
Hallett Walk. CT1 18 D2
Hanover Pl. CT2 18 B2
Harcourt Dri. CT2 18 A2
Harkness Dri. CT2 18 A1
Havelock St. CT1 18 C3
Hawks La. CT1 18 B4
Hawthorn Av. CT2 18 D1
Heaton Rd. CT1 18 B5
High St. CT1 18 B3
High St, Northgate. CT1 18 C3
Hollow La. CT1 18 A5
Hollowmede. CT1 18 A5
Holm Oak Clo. CT1 18 C5
Honeywood Clo. CT1 18 D2
Hospital La. CT1 18 B4
Hudson Rd. CT1 18 D2
INDUSTRIAL ESTATES:
Wincheap Ind Est. CT1 18 A5
Iron Bar La. CT1 18 C4
Ivy La. CT1 18 C4
Ivy Ter. CT1 18 B5
Jackson Rd. CT1 18 A4
Jessica Mews. CT1 18 D2
Jewry La. CT1 18 B3
Juniper Clo. CT1 18 C6
Keyworth Mews. CT1 18 D2
King St. CT1 18 C3
Kings Park. CT1 18 D3
Kingsmead Rd. CT1 18 C2
Kirbys La. CT2 18 B3
Knotts La. CT1 18 C3
Knowlton Walk. CT1 18 D2
Lady Woottons Grn. CT1 18 C3
Lancaster Rd. CT1 18 B5
Lansdown Rd. CT1 18 C5
Lesley Av. CT1 18 C6
Leycroft Clo. CT2 18 B1
Lime Kiln Rd. CT1 18 B5
Lincoln Av. CT1 18 D5
Linden Gro. CT2 18 B3
Link La. CT1 18 C4
London Rd. CT2 18 A3
Long Acre Clo. CT2 18 A2
Long Market. CT1 18 C4
Longport. CT1 18 D4
Love La. CT1 18 C4
Lower Bridge St. CT1 18 C4
Lower Chantry La. CT1 18 D4
Lyndhurst Clo. CT2 18 A1
Magdalen Ct. CT1 18 D5
Maiden La. CT1 18 A5
Malthouse Rd. CT2 18 C2
Mandeville Rd. CT2 18 B2
Market Way. CT2 18 C1
Marlowe Av. CT1 18 B4
Martindale Clo. CT1 18 C5
Martyrs Field Rd. CT1 18 B5
Maynard Rd. CT1 18 A5
Mead Way. CT2 18 A3
Mercery La. CT1 18 C3
Military Rd. CT1 18 C3
Mill La. CT1 18 C3
Milton Rd. CT1 18 C5
Monastery St. CT1 18 C4
Monks Clo. CT2 18 C1
Nackington Rd. CT1 18 D6
New Dover Rd. CT1 18 D4
New Ruttington La. CT1 18 C2
New St. CT2 18 A3
New St, Martyrs Field. CT1 18 B5
New Town St. CT1 18 D2
Norfolk Rd. CT1 18 B5
Norman Rd. CT1 18 C5
North Holmes Rd. CT1 18 D3
North La. CT2 18 B3
Northgate. CT1 18 C3
Notley St. CT1 18 D2
Nunnery Fields. CT1 18 C5
Nunnery Rd. CT1 18 C5
Nursery Walk. CT2 18 A2
Oaten Hill. CT1 18 C4
Oaten Hill Pl. CT1 18 C4
Old Dover Rd. CT1 18 C4
Old Ruttington La. CT1 18 C3
Orange St. CT1 18 C3
Orchard St. CT2 18 A3
Orient Pl. CT2 18 B2
Oxford Rd. CT1 18 B5
Palace St. CT1 18 C3
Parham Rd. CT1 18 D1
Payton Mews. CT1 18 D2
Petchell Mews. CT1 18 D2
Pilgrims Way. CT1 18 D4
Pin Hill. CT1 18 B4
Pine Tree Av. CT2 18 A2
Pound La. CT1 18 B3
Pretoria Rd. CT1 18 D3
Princes Way. CT2 18 A3
Priory of St Jacob. CT1 18 A5
Prospect Pl. CT1 18 C5
Providence Row. CT1 18 A5
Puckle La. CT1 18 C5
Queens Av. CT2 18 A3
Ramsey Clo. CT2 18 A2
Randolph Clo. CT1 18 C5
Raymond Av. CT1 18 C5
Redwood Clo. CT2 18 A2
Regency Pl. CT1 18 D2
Remston Mews. CT1 18 D2
Rheims Way. CT1 18 B4
Rhodaus Clo. CT1 18 B5
Rhodaus Town. CT1 18 B4
Ringwood Clo. CT2 18 B1
Riverdale Rd. CT1 18 D1
Rochester Av. CT1 18 D5
Roper Clo. CT2 18 B2
Roper Rd. CT2 18 B2
Rose La. CT1 18 C4
Roseacre Clo. CT2 18 A2
Roselands Gdns. CT2 18 A1
Rosemary La. CT1 18 B4
Rushmead Clo. CT2 18 A2
Ryde St. CT2 18 A3
St Alphege La. CT1 18 C3
St Augustines Rd. CT1 18 D5
St Dunstans Clo. CT2 18 A2
St Dunstans St. CT2 18 A2
St Dunstans Ter. CT2 18 A3
St Edmunds Rd. CT1 18 B4
St Georges La. CT1 18 C4
St Georges Pl. CT1 18 C4
St Georges St. CT1 18 C3
St Georges Ter. CT1 18 C4
St Gregorys Rd. CT1 18 D3
St Jacobs Pl. CT1 18 A5
St Johns La. CT1 18 B4
St Johns Pl. CT1 18 C2
St Lawrence Clo. CT1 18 D5
St Lawrence Forstal. CT1 18 D6
St Lawrence Rd. CT1 18 D5
St Margarets St. CT1 18 B4
St Martins Av. CT1 18 D3
St Martins Pl. CT1 18 D3
St Martins Rd. CT1 18 D3
St Martins Ter. CT1 18 D3
St Marys St. CT1 18 B4
St Michaels Pl. CT2 18 B1
St Michaels Rd. CT2 18 B1
St Mildreds Pl. CT1 18 A5
St Peters Gro. CT1 18 B3
St Peters La. CT1 18 B3
St Peters Pl. CT1 18 B3
St Peters St. CT1 18 B3
St Radigunds Pl. CT1 18 C2
St Radigunds St. CT1 18 B3

St Stephens Clo. CT2 18 B2
St Stephens Ct. CT2 18 B2
St Stephens Footpath.
CT2 18 B1
St Stephens Grn. CT2 18 B1
St Stephens Hill. CT2 18 B1
St Stephens Rd. CT2 18 B1
Salisbury Rd. CT2 18 A1
Seymour Pl. CT1 18 A5
Shaftesbury Rd. CT2 18 B1
Shepherdsgate. CT2 18 B2
Simmonds Rd. CT1 18 A5
Somner Clo. CT2 18 A2
South Canterbury Rd.
CT1 18 D4
Spring La. CT1 18 D4
Stanmore Ct. CT1 18 D3
Starle Clo. CT1 18 D2
Station Road E. CT1 18 B4
Station Road W. CT2 18 B3
Stephenson Rd. CT2 18 B1
Stour St. CT1 18 B4
Stuart Ct. CT1 18 C5
Stuppington La. CT1 18 B6
Sturry Rd. CT1 18 D2
Sun St. CT1 18 C3
Teddington Clo. CT1 18 D2
Temple Rd. CT2 18 A3
The Borough. CT1 18 C3
The Causeway. CT1 18 B2
The Drive. CT1 18 D6
The Friars. CT1 18 B3
The Gap. CT1 18 D6
The Hoystings Clo. CT1 18 C5
The Ness. CT1 18 D6
The Paddock. CT1 18 D4
Tourtel Rd. CT2 18 D2
Tower Way. CT1 18 B3
Tudor Rd. CT1 18 B5
Union Pl. CT1 18 C2
Union St. CT1 18 C2
Upper Bridge St. CT1 18 C4
Upper Chantry La. CT1 18 C4
Valley Rd. CT1 18 A5
Vernon Pl. CT1 18 C5
Verwood Clo. CT2 18 A1
Victoria Rd. CT1 18 A5
Victoria Row. CT1 18 C3
Wacher Clo. CT2 18 B1
Watling St. CT1 18 B4
West Pl. CT2 18 A2
Westgate Ct Av. CT2 18 A2
Westgate Gro. CT2 18 B3
Westgate Hall Rd. CT1 18 B3
White Horse La. CT1 18 B3
Whitehall Bridge Rd.
CT2 18 A3
Whitehall Rd. CT2 18 A3
Whitehall Gdns. CT2 18 A3
Whitehall Rd. CT2 18 A4
Whitstable Rd. CT2 18 A3
Willow Clo. CT2 18 D1
Wincheap. CT1 18 A5
Winchester Gdns. CT1 18 C5
Woodville Clo. CT1 18 A6
York Rd. CT1 18 B5
Zealand Rd. CT1 18 B5

CHARING

Ashford Rd. TN27 19 C3
Burleigh Rd. TN27 19 B3
Canterbury Rd. TN27 19 B1
Centenary Ct. TN27 19 C2
Church La. TN27 19 C2
Clearmount Dri. TN27 19 C1
Downs Clo. TN27 19 C2
Downs Way. TN27 19 C2
Haffenden Mdw. TN27 19 B2
Hither Field. TN27 19 B3
Hook La. TN27 19 A2
Maidstone Rd. TN27 19 A1
Monks Walk. TN27 19 C2
Old Ashford Rd. TN27 19 C2
Pett La. TN27 19 C2
Pilgrims Ct. TN27 19 C2
Pilgrims Way. TN27 19 D1
Pluckley Rd. TN27 19 B3
Pym Ho. TN27 19 C2
Sayer Rd. TN27 19 B1
School Rd. TN27 19 B2
Station Rd. TN27 19 B3
The Glebe. TN27 19 C2
The High St. TN27 19 C2
The Hill. TN27 19 C2

The Moat. TN27 19 C2
The Wynd. TN27 19 C1
Toll La. TN27 19 D3
Westwell La. TN27 19 D3
Wheeler Rd. TN27 19 B2
Woodbrook. TN27 19 C2

CHATHAM

Admirals Walk. ME4 20 B1
Afghan Rd. ME4 20 A5
Albany Rd. ME4 20 D6
Albany Ter. ME4 20 B4
Albert Rd. ME4 20 C6
Amherst Hill. ME7 20 C3
Amherst Redoubt. ME7 20 C3
Anchor Wharf. ME4 20 B2
Anthony Way. ME2 20 A1
Armada Way. ME4 20 B5
Arnolde Clo. ME4 20 A2
Athelstan Rd. ME4 20 B6
Baffin Clo. ME4 20 C6
Bank St. ME4 20 D5
*Barfleur Manor,
Middle St. ME7 20 C2
Barnard Ct. ME4 20 C2
Barrier Rd. ME4 20 B3
Batchelor St. ME4 20 C4
Bath Hard La. ME1 20 A4
Beaconsfield Rd. ME4 20 B6
Beaufort St. ME4 20 A2
Beaufort Park. ME2 20 A3
Best St. ME4 20 B4
Bingley Rd. ME1 20 A4
Blenheim Av. ME4 20 A6
Booth Rd. ME4 20 B6
Boundary Rd. ME4 20 A6
Brenchley Clo. ME1 20 A6
Bright Rd. ME4 20 D6
Brisbane Rd. ME4 20 C5
Brompton Clo. ME4 20 B2
Brompton Hill. ME4 20 B2
Brompton Rd. ME4 20 D2
Bryant Av. ME4 20 C5
Buller Rd. ME4 20 C6
Cambridge Ter. ME4 20 B4
Carpeaux Clo. ME4 20 C4
Carpenters Clo. ME1 20 A6
Castle Rd. ME4 20 D6
Central Av. ME4 20 C1
Central Pk Gdns. ME4 20 A6
Chalk Pit Hill. ME4 20 C5
Chamberlain Rd. ME4 20 D6
Charles St. ME4 20 A5
Charter St. ME4 20 B6
Chatham Hill. ME5 20 D5
Chaucer Clo. ME4 20 A1
Chelmer Rd. ME4 20 D5
Chilham Rd. ME4 20 B5
Church La. ME4 20 32
Church Path. ME7 20 D2
Church St. ME4 20 C4
City Way. ME1 20 A5
Claremont Way. ME4 20 C5
Clarence Rd. ME4 20 D6
Clipper Clo. ME2 20 A2
Clover St. ME4 20 B4
Cobden Rd. ME4 20 D6
College Av. ME7 20 C1
College Rd. ME4 20 C1
Constitution Hill. ME5 20 D5
Constitution Rd. ME5 20 D5
Conway Mews. ME7 20 C2
Corkwell St. ME4 20 A5
Cottall Av. ME4 20 B6
Cranleigh Gdns. ME4 20 A4
Cressey Ct. ME4 20 A4
Cromwell Ter. ME4 20 C5
Cross St. ME4 20 C4
Culpeper Clo. ME2 20 A2
Cumberland Rd. ME4 20 D1
Curzon Rd. ME4 20 C6
Dagmar Rd. ME4 20 D6
Dale St. ME4 20 B6
Dickens Rd. ME2 20 A1
Dock Rd. ME4 20 B3
East Rd. ME4 20 C1
East St. ME4 20 C4
Edward St. ME4 20 D5
Eldon St. ME4 20 C4
Elmhurst Gdns. ME4 20 A5
Enterprise Clo. ME2 20 A1
Ernest Rd. ME4 20 C6
Fieldworks Rd. ME7 20 C1
Five Bells La. ME1 20 A4

Flaxmans Ct. ME7 20 C2
Fort Pitt Hill. ME4 20 A4
Fort Pitt St. ME4 20 A5
Frederick St. ME4 20 C5
Garden St. ME7 20 C2
Gerald Av. ME4 20 C6
Gibraltar Av. ME7 20 C2
Gibraltar Hill. ME4 20 B4
Gills Cottages. ME1 20 A4
Gills Ct. ME4 20 A1
Ginsbury Clo. ME2 20 A2
Gladstone Rd. ME4 20 A6
Glencoe Rd. ME4 20 C6
Globe La. ME4 20 B4
Gordon Rd,
Brompton. ME7 20 C1
Gordon Rd,
Chatham. ME4 20 C6
Graham Clo. ME4 20 C2
Grange Hill. ME5 20 D5
Great Lines. ME7 20 C3
Grosvenor Av. ME4 20 A5
Grove Rd. ME4 20 D6
Gundulph Rd. ME4 20 A4
Haig Av. ME4 20 C6
Hamond Hill. ME4 20 B4
Hards Town. ME4 20 C4
Hare St. ME4 20 D5
Hartington St. ME4 20 C5
Hawkins Clo. ME4 20 C2
Haymen St. ME4 20 A5
Henry St. ME4 20 D5
Herbert Rd. ME4 20 C5
Herman Ter. ME4 20 C5
Higgins La. ME4 20 B4
High St,
Brompton. ME4 20 C2
High St,
Chatham. ME4 20 B4
Hilda Rd. ME4 20 C5
Hillcrest Rd. ME4 20 B6
Hills Ter. ME4 20 B5
Hillside Rd. ME4 20 C5
Holcombe Rd. ME4 20 B6
Hope St. ME4 20 C5
Hospital La. ME1 20 A4
INDUSTRIAL ESTATES:
Arden Business Pk.
ME2 20 A1
Central Business Pk.
ME2 20 A1
Henley Business Pk.
ME2 20 A1
Lakeside Pk. ME2 20 A2
Meridian Pk. ME2 20 A2
Neptune Business Est.
ME2 20 A1
Riverside Est. ME2 20 A3
Riverside One. ME2 20 A1
Riverside Three. ME2 20 A2
Riverside Two. ME2 20 B2
Sextant Park. ME2 20 A1
Victory Business Pk.
ME2 20 A1
Ingle Rd. ME4 20 B6
Institute Rd. ME4 20 C5
James St. ME4 20 B4
Jenkins Dale. ME4 20 B5
Jeyes St. ME4 20 C5
Keyes Av. ME4 20 C6
Khartoum Rd. ME7 20 B3
Khyber Rd. ME4 20 C1
King Edward Rd. ME4 20 B6
King St. ME4 20 C4
Kings Bastion. ME7 20 C3
Kingswood Av. ME4 20 B6
Lakeside Ct. ME2 20 A2
Lansdowne Rd. ME4 20 A6
Laser Quay. ME4 20 A2
Leitch Row. ME7 20 C2
Lendrim Clo. ME7 20 C2
Lennox Row. ME7 20 C2
Leopold Rd. ME4 20 C5
Lester Rd. ME4 20 C5
Lines Ter. ME4 20 C4
Listmas Rd. ME4 20 D5
Longhill Av. ME5 20 D5
Lumsden Ter. ME4 20 A4
Luton Rd. ME4 20 D5
Magpie Hall Rd. ME4 20 C6
Maida Rd. ME4 20 D6
Maidstone Rd. ME4 20 B6
Main Gate Rd. ME4 20 B2
Manor Rd. ME4 20 B4
Manor St. ME7 20 C2
Mansion Row. ME7 20 C2
Marc Brunel Way. ME4 20 C1

Marlborough Rd. ME7 20 D4
Maxwell Rd. ME4 20 C3
May Ter. ME7 20 C2
McCudden Row. ME7 20 C2
Meadow Bank Rd.
ME4 20 D4
Medway Gdns. ME4 20 C1
Medway St. ME4 20 B4
Meeting Ho La. ME4 20 B4
Melbourne Rd. ME4 20 C5
Melville St. ME4 20 C2
Middle St. ME7 20 C2
Military Rd. ME4 20 B4
Mills Ter. ME4 20 C5
Mitchell Av. ME4 20 B6
Mount Pleasant. ME5 20 D5
Mount Rd. ME4 20 B5
Mozart Ct. ME4 20 A6
Natal Rd. ME4 20 C6
Neale St. ME4 20 B6
Neptune Clo. ME2 20 A1
Neville Rd. ME4 20 A6
New Covenant Pl. ME1 20 A4
New Cut. ME4 20 B4
New Rd. ME4 20 B4
New Rd Av. ME4 20 A4
New Stairs. ME4 20 B2
New St. ME4 20 B5
Newnham St. ME4 20 D5
North Rd. ME7 20 C1
Officers Rd. ME4 20 D1
Old Pattens La. ME1 20 A6
Old Rd. ME4 20 B4
Orchard Villas. ME4 20 B5
Ordnance St. ME4 20 A5
Ordnance Ter. ME4 20 B4
Otway St. ME4 20 C5
Otway Ter. ME4 20 C5
Pagitt St. ME4 20 A6
Palmerston Rd. ME4 20 B6
Parham Rd. ME4 20 B6
Pasley Rd. ME7 20 C2
Pasley Rd East. ME7 20 D1
Pasley Rd North. ME7 20 D1
Pasley Rd West. ME7 20 D1
Pattens Gdns. ME1 20 A6
Pattens La. ME4 20 A6
Perie Row. ME7 20 C2
Perry St. ME4 20 A5
Pleasant Row. ME7 20 C2
Port Rise. ME4 20 B5
Portland St. ME4 20 D6
Post Barn Rd. ME4 20 C6
Pretoria Rd. ME4 20 C6
Prince Arthur Av. ME7 20 D2
Princess Mary Av. ME4 20 D1
Prospect Row,
Brompton. ME7 20 C2
Prospect Row,
Chatham. ME4 20 C5
Purbeck Rd. ME4 20 B6
Queen St. ME4 20 C4
Railway St. ME4 20 C4
Redvers Rd. ME4 20 C6
Reform Rd. ME4 20 D6
Rhode St. ME4 20 C4
Richard St. ME4 20 B4
River St. ME7 20 C2
Rochester St. ME4 20 B5
Rope Walk. ME4 20 B3
Rosebery Rd. ME4 20 A6
Rowan Walk. ME4 20 A5
Royal Eagle Clo. ME2 20 A1
Royal Sovereign Av.
ME4 20 D1
Russell Ct. ME4 20 D5
Sailmakers Ct. ME4 20 D6
St Alban St. ME4 20 B5
St Bartholomews La.
ME1 20 A4
St Bartholomews Ter.
ME1 20 A4
St Leonards Av. ME4 20 B6
St Marys Gdns. ME4 20 D1
St Michaels Clo. ME4 20 B5
Salisbury Rd. ME4 20 C5
Sally Port Gdns. ME7 20 C2
Saunders St. ME4 20 B5
Sawyers Ct. ME4 20 D6
Scotteswood Av. ME4 20 B6
Scotts Ter. ME4 20 B5
Semple Gdns. ME4 20 A6
Seymour Rd. ME5 20 D5
Ship La. ME7 20 A4
Shipwrights Av. ME4 20 D6
Short St. ME4 20 D5
Silver Hill. ME4 20 B5

*Silver Hill Gdns,
Silver Hill. ME4 20 B5
Singapore Dri. ME7 20 C6
Sir Thomas Longley Rd.
ME2 20 A1
Skinner St. ME4 20 B5
Slicketts Hill. ME4 20 C5
Solomons Rd. ME4 20 C5
South Rd. ME4 20 D2
South Rd. ME7 20 C6
Southill Rd. ME4 20 B6
Springfield Ter. ME4 20 B6
Stoney Alley. ME4 20 C2
Sturla Rd. ME4 20 C6
Sunderland Quay.
ME2 20 A2
Sydney Rd. ME4 20 C6
Symons Av. ME4 20 C5
*Temeraire Manor,
Middle St. ME7 20 C2
The Brook. ME4 20 B5
The Chase. ME4 20 A6
The Mount. ME4 20 B5
The Paddock. ME4 20 B6
The Sally Port. ME7 20 C2
The Terrace. ME4 20 C5
Thorold Rd. ME5 20 D5
Trident Clo. ME4 20 A5
Union St. ME4 20 C2
Upbury Way. ME4 20 C2
Upper Britton Pl. ME7 20 D2
Upper East Rd. ME4 20 D2
Victoria Rd. ME4 20 D2
*Victory Manor,
Middle St. ME7 20 C2
Waghorn St. ME4 20 D5
Warner St. ME4 20 B5
Waterside St. ME2 20 A2
Watts St. ME4 20 B5
West Rd. ME4 20 C6
Westcourt St. ME7 20 C2
Westmount Av. ME4 20 B6
Whiffens Av. ME4 20 C2
Whiffens Av West.
ME4 20 C2
White Rd. ME4 20 C6
Whitehorse Hill. ME5 20 D6
Whitewall Rd. ME2 20 A2
Whitewall Way. ME2 20 A2
Whittaker St. ME4 20 C6
Windsor Av. ME4 20 B6
Wood St. ME7 20 C2
Wyndham Rd. ME4 20 A5
York Rd. ME7 20 D1

CLIFTONVILLE

Addiscombe Rd. CT9 21 A2
Adisham Way. CT9 21 C1
Airedale Clo. CT9 21 A1
Albion Rd. CT9 21 A1
Alfred Rd. CT9 21 B1
Amherst Clo. CT9 21 C2
Appledore Clo. CT9 21 C1
Approach Rd. CT9 21 A2
Arlington Gdns. CT9 21 C1
Arthur Rd. CT9 21 B1
Arundal Rd. CT9 21 B1
Athelstan Rd. CT9 21 A1
Avenue Gdns. CT9 21 C1
Balcomb Cres. CT9 21 C2
Bath Pl. CT9 21 A1
Beresford Gdns. CT9 21 C1
*Biddenden Clo,
Adisham Way. CT9 21 C1
Booth Pl. CT9 21 C1
Broadley Rd. CT9 21 C1
Brockley Rd. CT9 21 A1
Byron Av. CT9 21 A1
Caroline Sq. CT9 21 A1
Cedar Clo. CT9 21 B1
Clarence Av. CT9 21 D1
Clarendon Rd. CT9 21 A1
Cliff Ter. CT9 21 A1
Clifton Gdns. CT9 21 A1
Clifton Pl. CT9 21 A1
Clifton Rd. CT9 21 A1
Cliftonville Av. CT9 21 A1
Cliftonville Mews. CT9 21 A1
College Rd. CT9 21 A1
Cornwall Gdns. CT9 21 B1
Cowley Rise. CT9 21 C1
Crawford Gdns. CT9 21 C1
Cudham Gdns. CT9 21 D1
Cumberland Rd. CT9 21 C1

CRANBROOK

DARTFORD

DEAL

Canute Walk. CT14 24 B1
Capstan Row. CT14 24 C3
Castle Walk. CT14 24 C1
Century Walk. CT14 24 B4
Chapel St. CT14 24 C4
Church La. CT14 24 A5
Church Path. CT14 24 A5
Clanwilliam Rd. CT14 24 C5
Claremont Rd. CT14 24 A6
Clarence Pl. CT14 24 C4
College Rd. CT14 24 B2
Coppin St. CT14 24 C4
Courtney Rd. CT14 24 B2
Cowper Rd. CT14 24 A5
Deal Castle Rd. CT14 24 B4
Deal Rd. CT14 24 A5
Dibden Rd. CT14 24 C3
Dola Av. CT14 24 A5
Dolphin Sq. CT14 24 C3
Douglas Ter. CT14 24 B6
Duke St. CT14 24 B4
Enfield Rd. CT14 24 C3
Ethelbert Rd. CT14 24 B1
Exchange St. CT14 24 B4
Farrier St. CT14 24 C4
Garden Walk. CT14 24 B3
George All. CT14 24 C4
George St. CT14 24 C3
Gilford Rd. CT14 24 B6
Gladstone Rd. CT14 24 B6
Godwyn Rd. CT14 24 B1
Golden St. CT14 24 C4
Golf Rd. CT14 24 B1
Golf Road Pl. CT14 24 B2
Grange Rd. CT14 24 A5
Granville St. CT14 24 B6
Griffin Clo. CT14 24 C3
Harold Rd. CT14 24 B2
Hengist Rd. CT14 24 C3
High St. CT14 24 C3
Homefield. CT14 24 A4
Hope Rd. CT14 24 B6
Horsa Rd. CT14 24 C2
Ivy Pl. CT14 24 C4
Jernon Pl. CT14 24 C1
King Edward Av. CT14 24 B1
King St. CT14 24 C4
Lanfranc Rd. CT14 24 B2
Langton Clo. CT14 24 B2
Leas Rd. CT14 24 A6
Links Rd. CT14 24 B2
Lister Clo. CT14 24 A6
London Rd. CT14 24 C6
Marine Rd. CT14 24 C6
Market St. CT14 24 C4
Matthews Clo. CT14 24 B4
Middle St. CT14 24 C4
Mill Rd. CT14 24 A6
Miller Clo. CT14 24 B2
Nelson St. CT14 24 B3
New St. CT14 24 C4
North Ct. CT14 24 B4
North Lea. CT14 24 B3
North St. CT14 24 C4
Northcote Rd. CT14 24 C5
Northwall Ct. CT14 24 B4
Northwall Mews. CT14 24 B3
Northwall Rd. CT14 24 A2
Oak St. CT14 24 C4
Park Av. CT14 24 A6
Park Lea. CT14 24 A6
Park St. CT14 24 B5
Pavilion Clo. CT14 24 B2
Peter St. CT14 24 B3
Portobello St. CT14 24 C3
Prince of Wales Ter. CT14 24 C5
Princes St. CT14 24 B3
Queen St. CT14 24 B5
Queens Mews. CT14 24 B5
Ranelagh Rd. CT14 24 C6
Ravenscourt Rd. CT14 24 B6
Redhouse Wall. CT14 24 A1
Roberts St. CT14 24 B3
Roman Clo. CT14 24 A5
St Andrews Rd. CT14 24 B4
St Davids Rd. CT14 24 B4
St Georges Rd. CT14 24 B4
St Georges Pass. CT14 24 C4
St Leonards Rd. CT14 24 A6
St Patricks Clo. CT14 24 B4
St Patricks Rd. CT14 24 B4
Sandown Clo. CT14 24 B1
Sandown Rd. CT14 24 C1
Saxon Pl. CT14 24 C3
Silver St. CT14 24 C3
Sondes Rd. CT14 24 C5

Souberg Clo. CT14 24 B2
South Ct. CT14 24 C5
South Par. CT14 24 C4
South St. CT14 24 C5
South Wall. CT14 24 A4
Southwall Rd. CT14 24 A4
Stanhope Rd. CT14 24 B4
Stanley Rd. CT14 24 C4
Sutherland Rd. CT14 24 A5
Sydenham Rd. CT14 24 C3
Tar Path. CT14 24 A5
The Avenue. CT14 24 B4
The Drive. CT14 24 B6
The Fairway. CT14 24 B2
The Grove. CT14 24 A5
The Marina. CT14 24 C1
The Strand. CT14 24 C6
Union Rd. CT14 24 A5
Victoria Mews. CT14 24 B5
Victoria Par. CT14 24 C5
Victoria Rd. CT14 24 C6
Vlissingen Dri. CT14 24 B2
Walcheren Clo. CT14 24 B1
Wasterhout Clo. CT14 24 B1
Water St. CT14 24 B3
Wellington Rd. CT14 24 B5
West Lea. CT14 24 B3
West St. CT14 24 B4
Western Rd. CT14 24 B4
William Pitt Av. CT14 24 A5
Wilton Clo. CT14 24 A6
Young Clo. CT14 24 A4

DOVER

Adrian St. CT16 25 A4
Albany Pl. CT16 25 A4
Ashen Tree La. CT16 25 A3
Athol Ter. CT16 25 C3
Bench St. CT16 25 A4
Biggin St. CT16 25 A3
Cambridge Rd. CT16 25 A5
Cambridge Ter. CT16 25 A4
Camden Cres. CT16 25 A4
Cannon St. CT16 25 A3
Canons Gate Rd. CT16 25 B3
Castle Av. CT16 25 A2
Castle Hill Rd. CT16 25 B3
Castle St. CT16 25 A4
Castlemount Rd. CT16 25 A2
Chapel La. CT16 25 A4
Church St. CT16 25 A3
Clarence Pl. CT16 25 A6
Connaught Rd. CT16 25 A1
Constables Rd. CT16 25 B2
Cowgate Hill. CT16 25 A4
Deal Rd. CT16 25 B2
Dieu Stone La. CT16 25 A3
Dolphin La. CT16 25 A4
Dolphin Pl. CT16 25 A4
Douro Pl. CT16 25 B4
East Cliff. CT16 25 C3
East Norman Rd. CT16 25 B3
East Roman Ditch. CT16 25 B2
Eastbrook Pl. CT16 25 A3
Esplanade. CT16 25 A5
Fishmongers La. CT16 25 A4
Flyinghorse La. CT16 25 A4
Fort Burgoyne Rd. CT16 25 B1
Gaol La. CT16 25 A4
Godwin Rd. CT16 25 C3
Godwyne Clo. CT16 25 A2
Godwyne Path. CT16 25 A2
Godwyne Rd. CT16 25 A2
Harold Pass. CT16 25 A3
Harold St. CT16 25 A2
Harolds Rd. CT16 25 B2
Jubilee Way. CT16 25 C2
King St. CT16 25 A4
Knights Rd. CT16 25 B3
Laureston Pl. CT16 25 B3
Leyburne Rd. CT16 25 A2
Lord Warden Sq. CT16 25 A6
Maison Dieu Rd. CT16 25 A3
Marine Par. CT16 25 C3
Market Sq. CT16 25 A4
Market St. CT16 25 A4
Mill La. CT16 25 A4
Mortimer Rd. CT16 25 B3
New Bridge. CT16 25 B4
New St. CT16 25 A3
Old St Margarets Rd. CT16 25 C1

Pencester Rd. CT16 25 A3
Promenade. CT16 25 B4
Queen Elizabeth Rd. CT16 25 C4
Queen St. CT16 25 A4
Queens Gdns. CT16 25 A3
Russell St. CT16 25 A3
St James St. CT16 25 A4
St Marys Pass. CT16 25 A3
Salisbury Rd. CT16 25 A2
Slip Pass. CT16 25 A4
Snargate St. CT16 25 A5
Stenbrook. CT16 25 A3
Taswell St. CT16 25 A3
The Gateway. CT16 25 B4
The Paddock. CT16 25 A3
Townwall St. CT16 25 A4
Union St. CT16 25 A5
Upper Rd. CT16 25 B2
Victoria Park. CT16 25 B3
Waterloo Cres. CT16 25 A5
Wellesley Rd. CT16 25 A4
West Norman Rd. CT16 25 B2
West Roman Ditch. CT16 25 C3
West Wing Rd. CT16 25 A1
Woolcomber St. CT16 25 B3
York St. CT16 25 A3

EDENBRIDGE

Albion Way. TN8 26 B2
Ash Clo. TN8 26 B5
Ashcombe Dri. TN8 26 B1
Barn Hawe. TN8 26 B4
Briar Clo. TN8 26 C3
Cedar Dri. TN8 26 B3
Chestnut Clo. TN8 26 B4
Church St. TN8 26 C5
Churchfield. TN8 26 C5
Clover Walk. TN8 26 C3
Commerce Way. TN8 26 B3
Coomb Field. TN8 26 B5
Croft Clo. TN8 26 C4
Croft La. TN8 26 C4
Crouch House Rd. TN8 26 A2
Crown Rd. TN8 26 C2
Enterprise Way. TN8 26 B2
Fairmead Rd. TN8 26 B1
Farmstead Dri. TN8 26 C2
Field Dri. TN8 26 B2
Fircroft Way. TN8 26 B2
Forge Croft. TN8 26 C4
Four Elms Rd. TN8 26 B3
Foxglove Clo. TN8 26 C3
Frantfield. TN8 26 C4
Grange Clo. TN8 26 C4
Great Mead. TN8 26 B3
Greenfield. TN8 26 B4
Halland Ct. TN8 26 B4
Harrow Clo. TN8 26 C3
Hawthorn Clo. TN8 26 B3
Heron Clo. TN8 26 C3
Hever Rd. TN8 26 C5
High Fields Rd. TN8 26 C4
High St. TN8 26 C4
Hilders Clo. TN8 26 B1
Hilders La. TN8 26 A2
Hillcrest Rd. TN8 26 B1
Homestead Rd. TN8 26 B1
Hopgarden Clo. TN8 26 C5
Katherine Rd. TN8 26 C5
Kestrel Clo. TN8 26 C3
Leather Market. TN8 26 C5
Lingfield Rd. TN8 26 A5
Lucilina Dri. TN8 26 B5
Lynmead Clo. TN8 26 B1
Magpie Grn. TN8 26 C3
Main Rd. TN8 26 B3
Mallard Way. TN8 26 C3
Manor House Gdns. TN8 26 B4
Manor Rd. TN8 26 B5
Marl Hurst. TN8 26 B2
Marlpit Clo. TN8 26 C6
Mead Rd. TN8 26 C6
Meadow La. TN8 26 C4
Mill Hill. TN8 26 B6
Moles Mead. TN8 26 B3
Newhouse Ter. TN8 26 B1
Oakfield Rd. TN8 26 B1
Orchard Clo. TN8 26 A3
Orchard Dri. TN8 26 A3
Oxfield. TN8 26 C3
Park Av. TN8 26 B3

Park View. TN8 26 B4
Penlee Clo. TN8 26 C4
Pine Gro. TN8 26 B4
Pit La. TN8 26 B2
Plough Walk. TN8 26 C3
Plover Clo. TN8 26 C3
Queens Ct. TN8 26 C4
Ridge Way. TN8 26 C2
Riverside. TN8 26 C5
Riverside Ct. TN8 26 C5
Robyns Way. TN8 26 C5
Rowfield. TN8 26 C3
School Field. TN8 26 B3
Skeynes Rd. TN8 26 B5
Skinners La. TN8 26 C2
Smithyfield. TN8 26 C4
Sorrell Clo. TN8 26 B1
Spitals Cross Est. TN8 26 C2
Springfield Rd. TN8 26 B5
Stackfield. TN8 26 C3
Stanbridge Rd. TN8 26 B4
Stangrove Rd. TN8 26 B4
Station App. TN8 26 C4
Station Rd. TN8 26 B2
Stoneyfield. TN8 26 C3
Streatfeild. TN8 26 C5
Sunnyside. TN8 26 B2
Swan La. TN8 26 B1
Swan Ridge. TN8 26 C2
The Brownings. TN8 26 B5
The Limes. TN8 26 B5
The Plat. TN8 26 C5
The Square. TN8 26 C5
Victoria Clo. TN8 26 C6
Victoria Rd. TN8 26 C6
Wainhouse Clo. TN8 26 C3
Water Lakes. TN8 26 C6
Wayside Dri. TN8 26 C2
Wellingtonia Way. TN8 26 B3
Westways. TN8 26 B3
Woodland Dri. TN8 26 C2
Woodpecker Clo. TN8 26 C3

FAVERSHAM

Abbey Pl. ME13 27 D3
Abbey Rd. ME13 27 D3
Abbey St. ME13 27 D3
Albion Pl. ME13 27 C4
Aldred Rd. ME13 27 C5
Alexander Dri. ME13 27 B4
Arthur Salmon Clo. ME13 27 B4
Ashford Rd. ME13 27 C6
Athelstan Rd. ME13 27 B5
Athol Pl. ME13 27 A3
Bank St. ME13 27 C4
Barnes Clo. ME13 27 B3
Barnfield Rd. ME13 27 C3
Beaumont Davey Clo. ME13 27 C6
Beaumont Ter. ME13 27 D5
Beckett St. ME13 27 B4
Beech Clo. ME13 27 B4
Belmont Rd. ME13 27 C5
Belvedere Rd. ME13 27 D3
Bensted Gro. ME13 27 A4
Blaxland Clo. ME13 27 B3
Bramblehill Rd. ME13 27 C3
Brent Hill. ME13 27 C3
Brent Rd. ME13 27 C4
Bridge Rd. ME13 27 C3
Briton Rd. ME13 27 C5
Brogdale Rd. ME13 27 B6
Brook Rd. ME13 27 C3
Broomfield Rd. ME13 27 C3
Bysing Wood Rd. ME13 27 A3
Cambridge Rd. ME13 27 B5
Canute Rd. ME13 27 C5
Capel Rd. ME13 27 B5
Caslocke St. ME13 27 C4
Cavour Rd. ME13 27 C4
Chapel La. ME13 27 D5
Chart Clo. ME13 27 B4
Church Rd. ME13 27 B1
Church St. ME13 27 D4
Churchill Way. ME13 27 B3
Cobb Walk. ME13 27 B3
Cobham Chase. ME13 27 B4
Colegates Clo. ME13 27 B1
Colegates Rd. ME13 27 A2
Conduit St. ME13 27 C4
Court St. ME13 27 D4
Cremer Pl. ME13 27 B3

Crescent Rd. ME13 27
Cress Way. ME13 27
Crispin Clo. ME13 27
Cross La. ME13 27
Curtis Way. ME13 27
Cyprus Rd. ME13 27
Dan Dri. ME13 27
Dark Hill. ME13 27
Davington Hill. ME13 27
Dorset Pl. ME13 27
East St. ME13 27
Edith Rd. ME13 27
Egbert Rd. ME13 27
*Elliots Pl,
  St Marys Rd. ME13 27
Ethelbert Rd. ME13 27
*Ethelred Ct,
  Ethelbert Rd. ME13 27
Everard Way. ME13 27
Faversham Reach.
  ME13 27
Fielding St. ME13 27
Finlay Clo. ME13 27
Flood La. ME13 27
Forbes Rd. ME13 27
Forge Clo. ME13 27
Forstall Rd. ME13 27
Front Brents. ME13 27
Garfield Pl. ME13 27
Gatefield La. ME13 27
Giraud Dri. ME13 27
Goldfinch Clo. ME13 27
Granville Clo. ME13 27
Greenway. ME13 27
Grove Clo. ME13 27
Grove Pl. ME13 27
Ham Rd. ME13 27
Harold Rd. ME13 27
Harrison Ter. ME13 27
Hatch St. ME13 27
Hazebrouk Rd. ME13 27
Horsford Walk. ME13 27
Hugh Pl. ME13 27
Institute Rd. ME13 27
Ivory Clo. ME13 27
John Hall Clo. ME13 27
Johnson Ct. ME13 27
Judd Rd. ME13 27
Kennedy Clo. ME13 27
Kiln Ct. ME13 27
Kings Rd. ME13 27
Kingsnorth Rd. ME13 27
Lammas Gate. ME13 27
Larksfield Rd. ME13 27
Lewis Clo. ME13 27
Lion Field. ME13 27
Lion Yard. ME13 27
London Rd. ME13 27
Lower Rd. ME13 27
Maitland Ct. ME13 27
Makenade Av. ME13 27
Market Pl. ME13 27
Middle Row. ME13 27
Millstream Clo. ME13 27
Monks Clo. ME13 27
Mount Field. ME13 27
Mount Pleasant. ME13 27
Mutton La. ME13 27
Napleton Rd. ME13 27
Nelson St. ME13 27
Newton Rd. ME13 27
Nightingale Rd. ME13 27
Nobel Ct. ME13 27
Norman Rd. ME13 27
North La. ME13 27
Oare Rd. ME13 27
Old Gate Rd. ME13 27
Orchard Pl. ME13 27
Ospringe Pl. ME13 27
Ospringe Rd. ME13 27
Ospringe St. ME13 27
Park Rd. ME13 27
Partridge La. ME13 27
Penshurst Rise. ME13 27
Plantation Rd. ME13 27
Preston Gro. ME13 27
Preston Park. ME13 27
Preston St. ME13 27
Priory Pl. ME13 27
Priory Rd. ME13 27
Priory Row. ME13 27
Quay La. ME13 27
Queens Rd. ME13 27
Reedland Cres. ME13 27
Roman Rd. ME13 27
Russell Pl. ME13 27

Anns Rd. ME13 27 B5
Catherines Dri.
 ME13 27 D5
Johns Rd. ME13 27 D5
Marys Rd. ME13 27 D5
Nicholas Rd. ME13 27 A4
Pauls La. ME13 27 A4
Peters Ct. ME13 27 A5
hool Rd. ME13 27 D6
xon Rd. ME13 27 C5
ager Rd. ME13 27 B2
venacre Rd. ME13 27 C3
eerways. ME13 27 C3
erwood Clo. ME13 27 B3
nack Alley. ME13 27 D3
ephens Clo. ME13 27 D5
lomans La. ME13 27 D5
uth Rd. ME13 27 C4
illett Clo. ME13 27 B5
ringhead Rd. ME13 27 C4
table Ct,
 St Marys Rd. ME13 27 D5
ation Rd. ME13 27 D5
nebridge Way.
 ME13 27 B4
onedane Ct. ME13 27 C3
mpter Way. ME13 27 C4
nners St. ME13 27 C4
e Close. ME13 27 C5
e Knole. ME13 27 B4
Larches. ME13 27 A3
e Leas. ME13 27 B3
e Mall. ME13 27 C5
e Maltings. ME13 27 D3
omas Rd. ME13 27 C4
ion St. ME13 27 C5
per Brents. ME13 27 D3
per St Anns Rd.
 ME13 27 B5
arage La. ME13 27 A6
arage St. ME13 27 D4
ctoria Pl. ME13 27 C5
allers Rd. ME13 27 A5
ater La. ME13 27 C4
ater La,
Ospringe. ME13 27 A6
ells Way. ME13 27 B3
est St. ME13 27 A4
estern Link. ME13 27 A4
niting Cres. ME13 27 A3
ldish Rd. ME13 27 A3
llement Rd. ME13 27 B4
lliam St. ME13 27 D5
llow Av. ME13 27 A4
oodgate Clo. ME13 27 B3
eights Ct. ME13 27 B2

FOLKESTONE

bott Rd. CT20 28 C2
ert Rd. CT19 28 A1
ion Rd. CT19 28 B1
ion Villas. CT20 28 B1
exandra Gdns. CT20 28 A4
exandra St. CT19 28 C1
cher Rd. CT19 28 B1
thur St. CT19 28 B1
h Tree Rd. CT19 28 C1
ldwin Ter. CT19 28 B1
yle St. CT20 28 B3
each St. CT20 28 C4
llevue St. CT20 28 B2
ack Bull Rd. CT19 28 A2
lton Rd. CT20 28 B1
nsor Rd. CT19 28 A1
scombe Rd. CT19 28 A2
urnemouth Gdns.
 CT19
urnemouth Rd. CT19 28 A2
uverie Pl. CT20 28 A4
uverie Sq. CT20 28 A4
adstone Av. CT19 28 A2
adstone New Rd.
 CT19
adstone Rd. CT19 28 B3
amblebown. CT19 28 B3
dge St. CT19 28 C1
rrow Rd. CT19 28 D2
mbridge Gdns. CT20 28 A3
mbridge Ter. CT20 28 C3
nterbury Rd. CT18 28 A3
arlotte St. CT20 28 B3
eriton Gdns. CT20 28 A3

Cheriton Pl. CT20 28 A4
Cheriton Rd. CT20 28 A3
Church St. CT20 28 B4
Clarence St. CT20 28 B3
Connaught Rd. CT20 28 A3
Coolinge La. CT20 28 A3
Copthall Gdns. CT20 28 A3
Coronation Par. CT20 28 D3
Darby Pl. CT20 28 A3
Darby Rd. CT20 28 A3
Darlington St. CT20 28 A3
Dawson Rd. CT19 28 B1
Denmark St. CT19 28 C1
Devon Rd. CT19 28 A2
Dover Rd. CT20 28 B3
Dudley Rd. CT19 28 C2
Dyke Rd. CT19 28 C3
East Cliff. CT19 28 C2
East Cliff Gdns. CT19 28 C3
East St. CT19 28 C3
Eastfields. CT19 28 B2
Edward Rd. CT19 28 A1
Elm Rd. CT19 28 C1
Elmstead Pl. CT20 28 C3
Ernwell Rd. CT19 28 B1
Fern Bank Cres. CT19 28 B1
Folly Rd. CT19 28 C1
Foord Rd. CT20 28 A2
Foreland Av. CT19 28 D1
Foresters Way. CT20 28 A3
Garden Rd. CT19 28 A1
Gladstone Rd. CT19 28 B1
Gloucester Pl. CT20 28 B3
Grace Hill. CT20 28 B3
Green La. CT19 28 B1
Grove Rd. CT20 28 B2
Guildhall St. CT20 28 B3
Harbour App Rd. CT20 28 C4
Harbour St. CT20 28 C3
Harbour Way. CT20 28 C3
Harvey St. CT20 28 B3
Hasborough Rd. CT19 28 D2
High St. CT20 28 B3
INDUSTRIAL ESTATES:
Highfield Ind Est.
 CT19 28 D1
James St. CT19 28 B1
Jesmond St. CT19 28 A1
Lawrence Ct. CT19 28 C1
Lennard Rd. CT20 28 C2
Linden Cres. CT19 28 B1
London St. CT20 28 C3
Longford Ter. CT20 28 A4
Lower Sandgate Rd.
 CT20 28 A5
Manor Rd. CT20 28 A4
Margaret St. CT20 28 B4
Marine Cres. CT20 28 B4
Marine Par. CT20 28 B4
Marine Prom. CT20 28 B5
Marine Ter. CT20 28 B4
Martello Rd. CT20 28 C2
Mead Rd. CT19 28 A1
Middleburg Sq. CT20 28 A4
Mill Bay. CT20 28 B3
Mill Field. CT20 28 B3
Morrison Rd. CT19 28 C1
Mount Pleasant Rd.
 CT20 28 B2
Myrtle Rd. CT19 28 B2
Neason Ct. CT19 28 B1
Neason Way. CT19 28 D1
New St. CT20 28 B3
North St. CT19 28 C3
Ormonde Rd. CT20 28 C2
Oxford Ter. CT20 28 A4
Palmerston St. CT19 28 A2
Park Farm Rd. CT19 28 A1
Pavilion Rd. CT19 28 A1
Payers Park. CT20 28 B2
Pembroke Ct. CT20 28 C1
Penfold Rd. CT19 28 C2
Peter St. CT2 28 B2
Pleydell Gdns. CT20 28 B3
Pound Way. CT20 28 B4
Princess St. CT20 28 B4
Priory Gdns. CT20 28 B4
Queen St. CT20 28 B3
Radnor Bri Rd. CT20 28 C2
Radnor Park Rd. CT19 28 A1
Rendezvous St. CT20 28 B3
Road of
 Remembrance. CT20 28 B4
Rossendale Gdns.
 CT20 28 C3
Rossendale Rd. CT20 28 C2
Russell Rd. CT19 28 A1

Ryland Pl. CT20 28 C2
St Eanswythes Way.
 CT20 28 B3
St Johns Church Rd.
 CT19 28 A2
St Johns St. CT20 28 B2
St Michaels St. CT20 28 B3
Sandgate Rd. CT20 28 A4
Seagrave Cres. CT19 28 D2
Seagrave Rd. CT19 28 D2
Shakespeare Ter. CT20 28 A4
Shellons St. CT20 28 A3
Shepway Clo. CT19 28 B2
Ship St. CT19 28 A2
Sidney St. CT19 28 B1
South St. CT20 28 C3
Southbourne Rd. CT19 28 C2
Stuart Rd. CT19 28 C2
Sussex Rd. CT19 28 A2
Telford Ct. CT19 28 B1
Thanet Gdns. CT19 28 D1
The Bayle. CT210 28 B4
The Durlocks. CT20 28 C3
The Leas. CT20 28 A5
The Parade. CT20 28 A5
The Stade. CT20 28 C3
The Tram Rd. CT20 28 C3
Tontine St. CT20 28 B3
Varne Pl. CT19 28 D2
Varne Rd. CT19 28 D2
Victoria Gro. CT20 28 A3
Victoria Rd. CT19 28 A2
Walton Rd. CT19 28 A1
Warren Clo. CT19 28 D1
Warren Rd. CT19 28 D1
Warren Way. CT19 28 D1
Watkin Rd. CT19 28 A1
Wear Bay Cres. CT19 28 D2
Wear Bay Rd. CT19 28 D3
West Cliff Gdns. CT20 28 A4
West Ter. CT20 28 A4

GILLINGHAM

Abbey Rd. ME8 29 D6
Acorn Rd. ME7 29 B6
Adelaide Rd. ME7 29 A5
Albany Rd. ME7 29 B4
Albany Rd. ME4 29 A6
Albany Ter. ME7 29 B4
Albert Rd. ME7 29 A4
Alexandra Av. ME7 29 C5
Ambrose Hill. ME5 29 A6
Annvera House. ME7 29 A2
Arden St. ME7 29 A3
Ash Tree La. ME5 29 B6
*Augusta Clo,
 Kelly Dri. ME7 29 A1
Austin Clo. ME75 29 C6
Avondale Rd. ME7 29 B3
Baden Rd. ME7 29 B2
Balmoral Rd. ME7 29 A4
Barnsole Rd. ME7 29 B4
Baron Clo. ME7 29 C2
Beacon Rd. ME5 29 A4
Beaconsfield Rd. ME7 29 C4
Beatty Av. ME7 29 D5
Beechwood Av. ME5 29 B6
Belmont Rd. ME7 29 A4
Beresford Rd. ME7 29 B4
Bluebell Clo. ME7 29 C3
Borough Rd. ME7 29 B5
Brasenose Av. ME7 29 B5
Bridge Rd. ME7 29 A1
Britton Farm St. ME7 29 A3
Britton St. ME7 29 A3
Broadway. ME8 29 D6
Brooklyn Paddock. ME7 29 B3
Buckingham Rd. ME7 29 B3
Burns Rd. ME7 29 A2
Burnt Oak Ter. ME7 29 A2
Buttermere Clo. ME7 29 D3
Byron Rd. ME7 29 A5
Camden Rd. ME7 29 B1
Canadian Av. ME7 29 C4
Canterbury St. ME7 29 A3
Carlton Av. ME7 29 C4
Castlemaine Av. ME7 29 C2
Cavendish Av. ME7 29 C3
Central Av. ME4 29 A4
Chada Av. ME7 29 C5
Charlton Manor. ME7 29 A3
Charter St. ME7 29 A3
Chatham Hill. ME5 29 A5
Chatsworth Rd. ME7 29 A2

Chaucer Rd. ME7 29 B5
Chester Rd. ME7 29 B6
Chicago Av. ME7 29 C4
Christmas St. ME7 29 C2
Church Hill. ME5 29 A6
Church Path. ME7 29 B2
Church St. ME7 29 C2
Cleave Rd. ME7 29 B6
Clifton Rd. ME7 29 A2
College Av. ME7 29 A4
Coniston Clo. ME7 29 D3
Connaught Rd. ME7 29 B3
Connaught Rd. ME4 29 A6
Constitution Rd. ME5 29 A6
Copenhagen Rd. ME7 29 A4
Cornwall Rd. ME7 29 C2
Cornwallis Av. ME7 29 D4
Coronation Rd. ME5 29 A6
Corporation Rd. ME7 29 B2
Corral Clo. ME5 29 B6
Coulman St. ME7 29 B4
Court Lodge Rd. ME7 29 D2
Cowper Rd. ME7 29 B5
Crosley Rd. ME7 29 B6
Cross St. ME7 29 A2
Crown St. ME7 29 A2
Cumberland Rd. ME4 29 A1
Cypress Ct. ME7 29 D3
Dalton St. ME7 29 A3
Darland Av. ME7 29 C4
Davenport Av. ME7 29 B2
Dawes St. ME7 29 A3
Derby Rd. ME5 29 C6
Devonshire Rd. ME7 29 B2
Dial Clo. ME7 29 D2
Dial Rd. ME7 29 D2
Duncan Rd. ME7 29 B4
East St. ME7 29 B2
Eastern Rd. ME7 29 D2
Edinburgh Rd. ME7 29 A5
Edinburgh Rd. ME5 29 A6
Elm Rd. ME7 29 C3
Eva Rd. ME7 29 B6
Exmouth Rd. ME7 29 A1
Ferndale Rd. ME7 29 C3
Firethorn Clo. ME7 29 C3
First Av. ME7 29 C6
Forge La. ME7 29 C2
Fourth Av. ME7 29 B4
Fox St. ME7 29 A2
Franklin Rd. ME7 29 B3
Frederick Rd. ME7 29 A4
Fresia Clo. ME7 29 C3
Gads Hill. ME7 29 D2
Gardner St. ME7 29 A3
Garfield Rd. ME7 29 A4
Gillingham Gate Rd.
 ME4 29 A1
Gillingham Grn. ME7 29 C2
Gillingham Rd. ME7 29 A4
Glanville Rd. ME7 29 B4
Glebe Rd. ME7 29 C5
Gordon Rd. ME7 29 B3
Gorst St. ME7 29 A3
Grange Rd. ME7 29 C2
Granville Rd. ME7 29 A3
Green St. ME7 29 A3
Greenfield Rd. ME7 29 B3
Haig Av. ME7 29 C4
Hamilton Rd. ME7 29 B2
Harold Av. ME7 29 C4
Hazlemere Dri. ME7 29 D3
Hewitt Clo. ME7 29 D2
High St. ME7 29 A3
Holly Clo. ME7 29 C2
Holmside. ME7 29 C6
Imperial Rd. ME7 29 A3
Ingram Rd. ME7 29 C3
James St. ME7 29 A3
Jeyes Rd. ME7 29 A4
Jezreels Rd. ME7 29 B6
Jubilee Ter. ME7 29 A2
Junction Rd. ME7 29 B5
Kelly Dri. ME7 29 A1
Kimberley Rd. ME7 29 B5
King Edward Rd. ME7 29 D2
King St. ME7 29 A3
King William Rd. ME7 29 A1
Kingswood Rd. ME7 29 B1
Knight Av. ME7 29 C2
Larkfield Av. ME7 29 C5
Latimer Pl. ME4 29 A1
Laurel Rd. ME7 29 A1
Lawrence St. ME7 29 A3
Layfield Rd. ME7 29 D2
Leet Clo. ME7 29 C3
Leslie Rd. ME7 29 B1

Lincoln Rd. ME7 29 B2
Linden Rd. ME7 29 C3
Livingstone Circus.
 ME7 29 B4
Livingstone Rd. ME7 29 B4
Lobelia Clo. ME7 29 C3
Lock St. ME7 29 A3
Longfellow Rd. ME7 29 A5
Louisville Av. ME7 29 C4
Lower East Rd. ME7 29 A1
Lower Woodlands Rd.
 ME7 29 D2
Luton Rd. ME4 29 A6
Macdonald Rd. ME7 29 B2
Maida Rd. ME4 29 A6
Malvern Rd. ME7 29 C6
Maple Av. ME7 29 C3
Marathon Paddock.
 ME7 29 B4
Margate Clo. ME7 29 C2
May Rd. ME7 29 A4
Maynard Pl. ME5 29 B6
Medway Rd. ME7 29 A1
Milburn Rd. ME7 29 A1
Mill Rd. ME7 29 A2
Milner Rd. ME7 29 B2
Milton Rd. ME7 29 A5
Montgomery Rd. ME7 29 A5
Montrose Av. ME5 29 C6
Napier Rd. ME7 29 B5
Nelson Rd. ME7 29 B4
Nile Rd. ME7 29 A4
Oak Av. ME7 29 C3
Osborn Rd. ME7 29 B3
Osprey Av. ME5 29 C6
Otway St. ME7 29 B2
Owens Way. ME7 29 D2
Oxford Rd. ME7 29 B5
Paget St. ME7 29 A3
Palace Ct. ME5 29 B6
Park Av. ME7 29 B6
Park Manor. ME7 29 A3
Parr Av. ME7 29 B2
Pier App Rd. ME7 29 B1
Pier Rd. ME7 29 B1
Poppy Clo. ME7 29 C3
Portland Rd. ME7 29 C3
Pretoria Rd. ME7 29 B5
Priestfield Rd. ME7 29 D6
Priory Ct. ME7 29 D6
Priory Rd. ME8 29 D6
Purser Way. ME4 29 A1
Queens Rd. ME7 29 A4
Railway St. ME7 29 B3
Rainham Rd. ME7 29 A6
Randolph Rd. ME7 29 A3
Redfern Av. ME7 29 C3
Regent Rd. ME7 29 A4
Richmond Rd. ME7 29 A2
Ridgeway. ME7 29 A5
Rock Av. ME7 29 A5
Rosebery Rd. ME7 29 B1
St Albans Clo. ME7 29 C2
St Andrews Rd. ME7 29 B1
St Barnabas Clo. ME7 29 B5
St Georges Rd. ME7 29 B1
St Johns Rd. ME7 29 B1
St Marys Rd. ME7 29 A2
Sappers Walk. ME7 29 A3
Saunders St. ME7 29 A3
Saxton St. ME7 29 A3
School Av. ME7 29 C4
Seaton Rd. ME7 29 B5
Seaview Rd. ME7 29 A4
Second Av. ME7 29 C5
Selbourne Rd. ME7 29 B2
Shakespeare Rd. ME7 29 A5
Shottenden Rd. ME7 29 B1
Sidney Rd. ME7 29 A1
Skinner St. ME7 29 A3
Speedwell Clo. ME7 29 C3
Springfield Rd. ME7 29 A2
Stafford St. ME7 29 A4
Stanley Rd. ME7 29 A2
Star Mill Ct. ME5 29 B6
Star Mill La. ME5 29 B6
Stopford Rd. ME7 29 A5
Strand App Rd. ME7 29 C1
Strover St. ME7 29 A3
Stuart Rd. ME7 29 B6
Sturdee Av. ME7 29 C4
Sugarloaf Hill. ME5 29 B6
Sunnymead Av. ME7 29 C3
Tangmere Clo. ME7 29 D3
Tennyson Rd. ME7 29 A5
The Vineries. ME7 29 C3
Theo Pl. ME7 29 A3

Third Av. ME7 29 C5
Toledo Paddock. ME7 29 B3
Toronto St. ME7 29 C4
Trafalgar St. ME7 29 A4
Trinity Rd. ME7 29 A2
Upper Luton Rd. ME5 29 A5
Valley Rd. ME7 29 C4
Vicarage Rd. ME7 29 A4
Victoria St. ME7 29 B3
Virginia Rd. ME7 29 A1
Waterloo Rd. ME7 29 A4
Waterside La. ME7 29 D2
Watling Av. ME7 29 B6
Watling St. ME7 29 B6
Wellington Rd. ME7 29 A4
West St. ME7 29 B3
Wharf Rd. ME7 29 A5
Windmill Rd. ME7 29 A5
Windsor Rd. ME7 29 B3
Woodlands Rd. ME7 29 D4
Wyles St. ME7 29 A1
York Av. ME7 29 A4
York Hill. ME4 29 A6

GRAVESEND

Aintree Clo. DA12 30 C5
Albert Murrey Clo. DA12 30 D2
Albion Rd. DA12 30 D2
Alfred Pl. DA11 30 A3
Alfred Rd. DA11 30 C4
All Saints Rd. DA11 30 D2
Allanbrooke. DA12 30 D2
Anglesea Centre. DA11 30 C1
Armoury Dri. DA12 30 D2
Arthur St. DA11 30 B2
Arthur St W. DA11 30 B2
Artillery Row. DA12 30 D2
Ascot Rd. DA12 30 C5
Ash Rd. DA12 30 D2
Augustine Rd. DA12 30 D2
Austin Rd. DA11 30 B3
Bader Walk. DA12 30 A5
Bakerhill Rd. DA11 30 A6
Bank St. DA12 30 C1
Barrack Row.DA11 30 C1
Bartlett St. DA11 30 B3
Bath St. DA11 30 C1
Beatrice Gdns. DA11 30 A4
Beaumont Dri. DA11 30 A2
Bedford Rd. DA11 30 B4
Belvedere Clo. DA12 30 D3
Bentley St. DA12 30 D1
Beresford Rd. DA11 30 A2
Berkley St. DA12 30 C1
Bernard St. DA12 30 C1
Bligh Rd. DA11 30 C1
Boucher Dri. DA11 30 A5
Bowers Av. DA11 30 A6
Brandon St. DA11 30 C2
*Brewhouse Yd,
 Queen St. DA12 30 C1
Bronte View. DA12 30 D3
Brook Rd. DA11 30 A3
Bucks Cross Rd. DA11 30 A5
Burch Rd. DA11 30 A1
Burnaby Rd. DA11 30 A2
Bycliffe Mews. DA11 30 B2
Bycliffe Ter. DA11 30 B2
Cambrian Gro. DA11 30 C2
Campbell Rd. DA11 30 A3
Canal Rd. DA12 30 D1
Cannon Walk. DA12 30 D2
Canterbury Rd. DA12 30 D4
Carters Row. DA11 30 A4
Cecil Rd. DA11 30 B3
Cedar Av. DA12 30 D6
Central Av. DA12 30 C4
Chadwick Clo. DA11 30 A4
Chalky Bank. DA11 30 B6
Cherrywood Dri. DA11 30 A6
Chestnut Clo. DA11 30 A1
Christchurch Cres. DA12 30 D6
Christchurch Rd. DA12 30 D3
Christian Fields Av. DA12 30 D6
Church St. DA11 30 C1
Churchill Rd. DA11 30 A3
Clarence Pl. DA11 30 C3
Clarence Row. DA12 30 C3
Clarendon Rd. DA12 30 D1
Clifton Rd. DA12 30 C2
Clifton Marine Par. DA11 30 A1

Clifton Rd. DA11 30 C1
Clive Rd. DA11 30 C1
Cobham St. DA11 30 C2
Coldharbour Rd. DA11 30 A4
Collington Clo. DA11 30 A2
Commercial Pl. DA11 30 D1
Constitution Hill. DA12 30 D3
Coombe Rd. DA12 30 D4
Coopers Rd. DA11 30 A3
Cornwell Av. DA12 30 D5
Cremorne Rd. DA11 30 A2
Crete Hall Rd. DA11 30 A1
Crooked La. DA12 30 C1
Cross La E. DA12 30 C4
Cross La W. DA11 30 C4
Cross Rd. DA11 30 A1
Cross St. DA12 30 D1
Cumberland Av. DA12 30 D2
Cutmore St. DA11 30 C2
Cygnet Gdns. DA11 30 A4
Darnley Rd. DA11 30 B3
Darnley St. DA11 30 C2
Dashwood Rd. DA11 30 33
Denholm Rd. DA11 30 A5
Dennis Rd. DA11 30 C5
Devonshire St. DA11 30 C3
Dogwood Clo. DA11 30 A6
Dover Rd E. DA11 30 A2
Dowding Walk. DA11 30 A5
Durndale La. DA11 30 A6
Earl Rd. DA11 30 A3
East Crescent Rd. DA12 30 D1
East Mill. DA11 30 B1
East Ter. DA12 30 D1
Echo Sq. DA12 30 D4
Edwin St. DA12 30 C2
Elizabeth Ct. DA11 30 B1
Elm Rd. DA12 30 D5
Elmfield Clo. DA11 30 C3
Essex Rd. DA11 30 B3
Everest Clo. DA11 30 A5
Farlow Rd. DA11 30 A5
Farmcroft. DA11 30 B4
Ferguson Av. DA12 30 D6
Ferndale Rd. DA11 30 B3
Fiveash Rd. DA11 30 A2
Fountain Walk. DA11 30 A1
Garden Row. DA11 30 A5
Garrick St. DA11 30 C1
Gatwick Rd. DA11 30 C5
Gibson Clo. DA11 30 A5
Gill Cres. DA11 30 B5
Glebe Rd. DA11 30 A3
Glen View. DA12 30 D3
Gloucester Rd. DA12 30 D6
Gordon Pl. DA11 30 D1
Gordon Prom E. DA12 30 D1
Grange Rd. DA11 30 B2
Grangeways Clo. DA11 30 A6
Granville Rd. DA11 30 A2
Greenhill Rd. DA11 30 A4
Grieves Rd. DA11 30 A5
Haig Gdns. DA12 30 D2
Harden Rd. DA11 30 A5
Hardy Av. DA11 30 A4
Harmer St. DA12 30 D1
Harris Clo. DA11 30 A5
Hartshill Rd. DA11 30 B4
Havelock Rd. DA11 30 A3
Hawkins Av. DA12 30 D6
Hawthorn Clo. DA12 30 D6
Haynes Rd. DA11 30 B5
High St. DA11 30 C1
Hillary Av. DA11 30 A5
Hillingdon Rd. DA11 30 C4
Hollybush Rd. DA12 30 D4
Home Mead. DA12 30 C2
Hookfields. DA11 30 A5
Hunt Rd. DA11 30 A5
INDUSTRIAL ESTATES:
 Imperial Business Park. DA11 30 B1
 Imperial Retail Pk. DA11 30 B1
Ivy Clo. DA12 30 D5
Jellicoe Av. DA12 30 D5
Joy Rd. DA12 30 D3
Jury St. DA11 30 C1
Kemsley Clo. DA11 30 A6
Kent Rd. DA11 30 B3
Khartoum Pl. DA12 30 D1
King St. DA12 30 C1
Kings Dri. DA12 30 C5
Kitchener Av. DA12 30 D5
Ladyfields. DA11 30 B6
Lanes La. DA11 30 B6
Lansdowne Pl. DA11 30 A3

Lansdowne Sq. DA11 30 A1
Laurel Av. DA12 30 D4
Lawrance Sq. DA11 30 B5
Leigh Rd. DA11 30 C4
Leith Park Rd. DA12 30 C3
Lennox Av. DA11 30 B1
Lennox Rd. DA11 30 B1
Lennox Rd E. DA11 30 B2
Lingfield Rd. DA11 30 A3
London Rd. DA11 30 A1
Lord St. DA12 30 C2
Love La. DA12 30 D2
Lynton Rd. DA11 30 B3
Lynton Rd Sth. DA12 30 B3
McMillan Clo. DA12 30 D6
Mallow Clo. DA11 30 A6
Malvina Av. DA12 30 C4
Manor Rd. DA12 30 C2
Maple Rd. DA12 30 D6
Marina Dri. DA12 30 A2
Marks Sq. DA11 30 A6
May Av. DA11 30 A3
Mayfield Rd. DA11 30 C4
Mead Rd. DA11 30 C4
Meadow Rd. DA11 30 B4
Milroy Av. DA11 30 A4
Milton Av. DA12 30 D3
Milton Pl. DA12 30 D1
Milton Rd. DA12 30 C1
Mulberry Rd. DA11 30 A6
Napier Rd. DA11 30 A3
Nelson Rd. DA11 30 A4
New House La. DA11 30 A5
New Rd. DA11 30 C1
New St. DA12 30 C1
New Swan Yd. DA12 30 C1
Newmans Rd. DA11 30 A4
Newton Abbot Rd. DA11 30 B4
Nightingale Clo. DA11 30 A6
Nine Elms Gr. DA11 30 B2
Normans Clo. DA11 30 B2
North St. DA12 30 C2
Northcote Rd. DA11 30 A3
Northridge Rd. DA12 30 D5
Oak Rd. DA12 30 D5
Oaklands Rd. DA11 30 A6
Old Manor Dri. DA12 30 D3
Old Road E. DA11 30 C3
Old Road W. DA11 30 A3
Ordnance Rd. DA12 30 D1
Overcliffe. DA11 30 B1
Packham Rd. DA11 30 A5
Park Av,
 Perry St. DA11 30 A3
Park Av,
 Windmill Hill. DA12 30 D3
Park Pl. DA12 30 D2
Park Rd. DA11 30 C3
Parrock Av. DA12 30 D3
Parrock Rd. DA12 30 D3
Parrock St. DA12 30 C1
Peacock St. DA12 30 D2
Pegasus Ct. DA12 30 D5
Pelham Rd. DA11 30 B3
Pelham Rd Sth. DA11 30 A3
Pelham Ter. DA11 30 A3
Perry St. DA11 30 A3
Peter St. DA12 30 C2
Pier Rd. DA11 30 A1
Pilots Pl. DA12 30 D1
Pinnocks Clo. DA11 30 C3
Poplar Av.' DA12 30 D6
Porchfield Clo. DA12 30 D4
Portland Av. DA12 30 C4
Portland Rd. DA12 30 C3
Princes Rd. DA12 30 D6
Princes St. DA11 30 C1
Queen St. DA12 30 C1
Queens Rd. DA12 30 D5
Railway Pl. DA12 30 C2
Ranelagh Gdns. DA11 30 A2
Rathmore Rd. DA11 30 C2
Ridgeway Av. DA12 30 C5
Rosebery Ct. DA11 30 B3
Rouge La. DA12 30 C3
Royal Pier Rd. DA12 30 C1
Saddington St. DA12 30 C2
St Andrews Rd. DA12 30 C2
St Clements Clo. DA11 30 A5
St Georges Shopping
 Centre. DA11 30 C1
St James Clo. DA11 30 B2
St James St. DA11 30 B1
St Margaret Rd. DA11 30 A4
St Marks Av. DA11 30 A2

St Marys Av. DA11 30 A2
St Marys Clo. DA11 30 D4
St Thomas's Av. DA11 30 C3
Salisbury Rd. DA11 30 A3
Sandy Bank Rd. DA12 30 C3
School Rd. DA12 30 D5
Seymour Rd. DA11 30 A4
Sharland Rd. DA12 30 D4
Shears Grn Ct. DA11 30 B5
Sheppey Pl. DA12 30 C2
Shrubbery Rd. DA12 30 D3
Singlewell Rd. DA11 30 C5
Smarts Rd. DA12 30 D4
Snelling Av. DA11 30 A4
Sorrel Way. DA11 30 A6
South Hill Rd. DA12 30 D3
South St. DA12 30 C2
Southfleet Rd. DA11 30 A4
Spencer St. DA11 30 B2
Spire Clo. DA12 30 C3
Spring Gro. DA12 30 C3
Stanbrook Rd. DA11 30 A3
Stone St. DA11 30 C1
Struttons Av. DA11 30 A4
Stuart Rd. DA11 30 B1
Sunning Hill. DA11 30 A4
Sun La. DA12 30 D4
Swallow Fields. DA11 30 A5
Tensing Av. DA11 30 A5
Terrace St. DA11 30 C1
Thames Way. DA11 30 A2
The Avenue. DA11 30 B3
The Crescent. DA11 30 B4
The Downage. DA11 30 B4
The Fairway. DA11 30 C4
The Grove. DA12 30 D2
The Parrock. DA12 30 D2
The Shore. DA11 30 A1
The Terrace. DA12 30 C1
Third Av. DA11 30 A3
Townfield Cnr. DA12 30 D3
Trafalgar Rd. DA11 30 B2
Tree Tops. DA12 30 C6
Trinity Rd. DA12 30 C4
Trosley Av. DA11 30 C4
Vauxhall Clo. DA11 30 A2
Victoria Av. DA12 30 C2
Victoria Rd. DA11 30 A3
Warrior Av. DA12 30 D6
Waterloo St. DA12 30 D2
Watling St. DA11 30 A6
Weavers Clo. DA11 30 B3
Wellington St. DA12 30 D2
West Crescent Rd. DA12 30 D1
West Mill. DA11 30 A1
West St. DA11 30 C1
Westcott Av. DA11 30 B5
Westhill Clo. DA12 30 C3
White Av. DA11 30 A5
Whitehill Par. DA12 30 D5
Whitehill Rd. DA12 30 D4
Wilfred St. DA12 30 C1
William St. DA12 30 C2
Windmill St. DA12 30 C1
Windsor Rd. DA12 30 C5
Wingfield Rd. DA12 30 C3
Woodfield Av. DA11 30 C3
Woodville Pl. DA12 30 C2
Wrotham Rd. DA11 30 B6
Wycliffe Rd. DA11 30 A3
York Rd. DA11 30 D5
Zion Pl. DA12 30 C2

GREENHITHE/SWANSCOMBE

Abbey Rd. DA9 31 C1
Admirals Walk. DA9 31 A1
Alamein Rd. DA10 31 F2
Albert Rd. DA10 31 F2
Alexander Rd. DA10 31 C1
Alkerden Rd. DA10 31 B2
All Saints Clo. DA10 31 E1
Alma Rd. DA10 31 E1
Ames Rd. DA10 31 E2
Austen Clo. DA9 31 B2
Bean Rd. DA9 31 A1
Beaton Clo. DA9 31 B1
Betsham Rd. DA10 31 E3
Bevans Clo. DA10 31 B2
Bodle Av. DA10 31 D2
Boleyn Way. DA10 31 E3
Breakneck Hill. DA9 31 B1
Broad Rd. DA10 31 D2

Broomfield Rd. DA10 31 D?
Bushfield Walk. DA10 31 D2
Butcher Walk. DA10 31 E2
Castle Rd. DA10 31 E2
Castle St. DA9 31 A?
Castle St. DA10 31 E2
Childs Cres. DA10 31 D.
Church Rd. DA10 31 E2
Craylands La. DA10 31 D?
Craylands Sq. DA10 31 D?
Crest View. DA9 31 A?
Dial Clo. DA9 31 C?
Durrant Way. DA10 31 D?
Eagles Rd. DA9 31 A
Eglington Rd. DA10 31 E2
Eynsford Rd. DA9 31 B?
Galley Hill Rd. DA10 31 E?
Gasson Rd. DA10 31 E2
Gilbert Clo. DA10 31 D2
Gunn Rd. DA10 31 D?
Harmer Rd. DA10 31 C?
Hasted Clo. DA9 31 C?
Hedge Place Rd 31 A.
Herbert Rd. DA10 31 F?
High St. DA10 31 E
Hillcrest Rd. DA10 31 A
Hope Rd. DA10 31 F
Ingress Gdns. DA9 31 C
Irving Walk. DA10 31 D
Ivy Bower Clo. DA9 31 A
Ivy Villas. DA9 31 A
Johnsons Way. DA9 31 B.
Jubilee Clo. DA9 31 C?
Kemsley Clo. DA9 31 B'
King Edward Rd. DA9 31 A
Knockhall Chase. DA9 31 B
Knockhall Rd. DA9 31 B'
Lane Av. DA9 31 B
Leonard Av. DA9 31 E.
Lewis Rd. DA10 31 E:
London Rd. DA10 31 A
Low Clo. DA9 31 A
Madden Clo. DA10 31 D
Manor Rd. DA10 31 D
Maritime Clo. DA9 31 B
Mayfield. DA10 31 D
Milton Rd. DA10 31 E
Milton St. DA10 31 D
Mitchell Walk. DA10 31 E
Moore Rd. DA10 31 E
Mounts Rd. DA9 31 B
Munford Dri. DA10 31 E
Orchard Rd. DA10 31 E
Park Rd. DA10 31 E
Park Ter. DA9 31 B
Pilgrims View. DA9 31 C
Port Av. DA9 31 B
Providence St. DA9 31 A
Rectory Rd. DA10 31 E
Riverview Rd. DA9 31 A
St Pauls Clo. DA10 31 E
St Peters Clo. DA10 31 E
Seymour Walk. DA10 31 B
Skippers Clo. DA9 31 B
Smugglers Walk. DA9 31 B
Southfield Rd. DA10 31 F
Spring Vale. DA9 31 B
Stanhope Rd. DA10 31 F
Stanley Rd. DA10 31 E
Starboard Av. DA9 31 B
Station Rd. DA9 31 A
Steele Av. DA10 31 A
Sun Rd. DA10 31 F
Swanscombe St. DA10 31 E
Sweyne Rd. DA10 31 E
The Avenue. DA9 31 B
The Crescent. DA9 31 B
The Grove. DA10 31 E
Trebble Rd. DA10 31 D
Valley Gdns. DA9 31 B
Valley View. DA9 31 B
Vernon Rd. DA10 31 F
Wakefield Rd. DA9 31 C
Wallace Gdns. DA10 31 D
Watling St. DA2 31 D
Western Cross Clo. DA9 31 B
Whites Clo. DA9 31 C
Woodland Way. DA9 31 A
Wright Clo. DA10 31 D

HADLOW

Appletons. TN11 19 C
Blackmans La. TN11 19 A
Bourne Grange La. TN11 19 A

roadway. TN11 19 B6
rook Fields. TN11 19 B5
room Waters. TN11 19 B4
arpenters La. TN11 19 A5
axton La. TN11 19 B5
emetery La. TN11 19 D6
hesfield Clo. TN11 19 C5
hurch St. TN11 19 B6
ourt La. TN11 19 C6
ray Ct. TN11 19 B5
reat Elms. TN11 19 D5
ailstone Clo. TN11 19 B5
igh St. TN11 19 B6
ope Av. TN11 19 B5
enward Ct. TN11 19 B5
eeds Ho Mews. TN11 19 B5
onewood Way. TN11 19 C1
Maidstone Rd. TN11 19 C5
Maltings Gdns. TN11 19 B5
Mill View. TN11 19 A5
almers Brook. TN11 19 C4
ark Villas. TN11 19 C4
chool La. TN11 19 B5
mithers Clo. TN11 19 B5
teers Pl. TN11 19 B4
ainter Rd. TN11 19 B5
he Cherry Orchard. TN11 19 B5
he Forstal. TN11 19 C6
he Freehold. TN11 19 C5
he Maltings. TN11 19 B5
he Paddock. TN11 19 B4
he Square. TN11 19 B5
oby Gdns. TN11 19 B5
onbridge Rd. TN11 19 A6
wyford Rd. TN11 19 B5
alley Dri. TN11 19 C1
ictoria Rd. TN11 19 C6
Water Slippe. TN11 19 A5

HAMSTREET

shford Rd. TN26 32 A1
ankside. TN26 32 A1
ourne La. TN26 32 A2
ourne Wood. TN26 32 A2
unkley Mdw. TN26 32 B2
arters Wood. TN26 32 B2
ock La. TN26 32 A2
otton Hill Walk. TN26 32 A2
ukes Mdw. TN26 32 A3
airfield Ter. TN26 32 A3
arm Rd. TN26 32 A3
amstreet Rd. TN26 32 B2
uince Orchard. TN26 32 A2
omney Marsh Rd. TN26 32 A2
omney Rd. TN26 32 A3
uckinge Rd. TN26 32 A2
t Marys Clo. TN26 32 A1
ne Street. TN26 32 A2
illage Way. TN26 32 A2
Willow Dri. TN26 32 A3

HARRIETSHAM

shford Rd. ME17 32 A5
hippendale Dri. ME17 32 B5
hurch La. ME17 32 C4
hurch Rd. ME17 32 C5
ourt Lodge La. ME17 32 C4
ricketers Clo. ME17 32 C5
alton Ct. ME17 32 C5
ownlands. ME17 32 C5
ast St. ME17 32 B5
airbourne La. ME17 32 B5
orge Meadow. ME17 32 B5
oddington La. ME17 32 A4
ook La. ME17 32 C4
ens Way. ME17 32 B5
akelands. ME17 32 C4
arley Rd. ME17 32 C4
ercer Dri. ME17 32 D4
orthdowns View. ME17 32 D4
ld Layne. ME17 32 C4
ilgrims Lakes. ME17 32 C4
uested Way. ME17 32 A5
ectory La. ME17 32 B5
t Welcumes Way. ME17 32 C4

Sandway Rd. ME17 32 C5
Station Rd. ME17 32 B4
Stede Hill. ME17 32 C4
Taylor Clo. ME17 32 B5
West St. ME17 32 A5

HAWKHURST

All Saints Rd. TN18 33 C2
Barretts Rd. TN18 33 B1
Basden Cotts. TN18 33 C1
Copthall Av. TN18 33 B2
Cranbrook Rd. TN18 33 C2
Dickens Way. TN18 33 C2
Dunlop Ct. TN18 33 B1
Eden Ct. TN18 33 B1
Fairview. TN18 33 B2
Fieldways. TN18 33 C2
Hammonds. TN18 33 C1
Hartnokes. TN18 33 B1
Heartenoak Rd. TN18 33 C1
High St. TN18 33 A1
Highfield Clo. TN18 33 C2
Highgate Hill. TN18 33 B2
Mercers. TN18 33 B2
Murton Neale Clo. TN18 33 C1
Northgrove Rd. TN18 33 B1
Oakfield. TN18 33 B1
Oaklands Rd. TN18 33 B2
Ockley La. TN18 33 B1
Ockley Rd. TN18 33 B1
Park Cotts. TN18 33 C1
Queens Ct. TN18 33 C1
Queens Rd. TN18 33 C1
Rye Rd. TN18 33 C2
School Ter. TN18 33 B1
Slip Mill Rd. TN18 33 A1
Sopers Rd. TN18 33 A1
Tates. TN18 33 B2
The Colonnade. TN18 33 B1
The Smugglers. TN18 33 C2
Theobalds. TN18 33 B1
Vale Rd. TN18 33 B1
Water La. TN18 33 D2
Western Av. TN18 33 B1
Western Rd. TN18 33 B1
Whites La. TN18 33 C1
Winchester Rd. TN18 33 B1
Woodbury Rd. TN18 33 B1

HEADCORN

Ashleigh Gdns. TN27 34 B2
Bank Fields. TN27 34 A2
Biddenden Rd. TN27 34 C3
Bramleys. TN27 34 B2
Brooklands. TN27 34 B2
Chaplin Dri. TN27 34 A2
Church Path. TN27 34 A2
Clerks Field. TN27 34 B2
Dawks Meadow. TN27 34 B2
Downs Clo. TN27 34 C2
Forge La. TN27 34 B2
Forge Meadows. TN27 34 C2
Gibbs Hill. TN27 34 C2
Gooseneck La. TN27 34 A2
Grigg La. TN27 34 C2
High St. TN27 34 B2
Hydes Orchard. TN27 34 C2
Kings Rd. TN27 34 B2
Kingsland Gro. TN27 34 C2
Knaves Acre. TN27 34 B2
Knights Way. TN27 34 B2
Knowles Gdns. TN27 34 C3
Lenham Rd. TN27 34 B2
Maidstone Rd. TN27 34 A1
Millbank. TN27 34 A1
Moat Rd. TN27 34 A2
New Rd. TN27 34 A2
North St. TN27 34 A2
Oak Farm Gdns. TN27 34 B1
Oak La. TN27 34 C3
Oakfields. TN27 34 B2
Orchard Glade. TN27 34 C3
Rushford Clo. TN27 34 C3
Sharps Field. TN27 34 C3
Sherway Clo. TN27 34 C3
Station App. TN27 34 B2
Station Rd. TN27 34 B2
Thatch Barn Rd. TN27 34 B2
Tollgate Pl. TN27 34 C3
Ulcombe Rd. TN27 34 B1

Uptons. TN27 34 B1
Wheeler St. TN27 34 C3
Youngs Pl. TN27 34 A1

HERNE BAY

Albany Dri. CT6 33 A3
Arkley Rd. CT6 33 C4
Ashtrees. CT6 33 D4
Avenue Rd. CT6 33 A3
Bank St. CT6 33 C3
Beach St. CT6 33 B3
Beacon Hill. CT6 33 D3
Beacon Rd. CT6 33 D3
Beacon Walk. CT6 33 D3
Beaumanor. CT6 33 C5
Belle Vue Rd. CT6 33 D3
Beltinge Rd. CT6 33 D3
Bognor Dri. CT6 33 A4
Bowes La. CT6 33 C5
Brunswick Sq. CT6 33 B3
Bullers Av. CT6 33 C5
Bullockstone Rd. CT6 33 A5
Burton Fields. CT6 33 B3
Canterbury Rd. CT6 33 C4
Cavendish Rd. CT6 33 C4
Cecil Park. CT6 33 C4
Cecil St. CT6 33 D4
Central Par. CT6 33 A3
Chapel St. CT6 33 C3
Charles St. CT6 33 C3
Cherry Gdns. CT6 33 B4
Clarence Rd. CT6 33 A3
Clarence St. CT6 33 B3
Cobblers Bri Rd. CT6 33 A4
Collard Clo. CT6 33 D4
Courtlands. CT6 33 D4
Cross St. CT6 33 A4
Darenth Clo. CT6 33 D5
Dence Clo. CT6 33 D3
Dence Park. CT6 33 D4
Dering Rd. CT6 33 B4
Dolphin St. CT6 33 B3
Douglas Rd. CT6 33 C4
Downs Park. CT6 33 D4
East Cliff Par. CT6 33 D3
East Gate Clo. CT6 33 D5
East St. CT6 33 C3
Eddington La. CT6 33 A5
Elizabeth Way. CT6 33 D5
Fernlea Av. CT6 33 A4
Fleetwood Av. CT6 33 A4
Gordon Rd. CT6 33 C4
Gosfield Rd. CT6 33 C5
Greenacres Clo. CT6 33 D5
Greenhill Rd. CT6 33 A4
Hadleigh Gdns. CT6 33 D3
Hanover Sq. CT6 33 C3
Hanover St. CT6 33 B3
Herne Av. CT6 33 D4
Herneville Gdns. CT6 33 D4
High St. CT6 33 B3
Hillborough Rd. CT6 33 D3
Hillbrow Av. CT6 33 D5
Hillcroft Rd. CT6 33 D5
Hilltop Rd. CT6 33 D3
Ivanhoe Rd. CT6 · 33 D4
Kingfisher Ct. CT6 33 B5
Kings Rd. CT6 33 B4
Lane End. CT6 33 A3
Leighville Dri. CT6 33 A4
Linden Av. CT6 33 A4
Links Clo. CT6 33 D5
Market St. CT6 33 B3
Mayfield Rd. CT6 33 D4
Mickleburgh Av. CT6 33 D4
Mickleburgh Hill. CT6 33 C4
Mill La. CT6 33 D5
Minster Dri. CT6 33 A4
Montague St. CT6 33 A3
Mortimer St. CT6 33 B3
New St. CT6 33 C3
North St. CT6 33 C3
Nurserylands. CT6 33 B5
Oakdale Rd. CT6 33 D5
Orchard Rd. CT6 33 D4
Oxenden Park Dri. CT6 33 A4
Oxenden Sq. CT6 33 A3
Oxenden St. CT6 33 A3
Park Rd. CT6 33 B4
Parsonage Rd. CT6 33 C5
Pettman Clo. CT6 33 D5
Pier Av. CT6 33 B3
Pier Chine. CT6 33 B3
Pigeon La. CT6 33 D5

Plenty Brook Dri. CT6 33 B5
Priory La. CT6 33 C5
Prospect Hill. CT6 33 C3
Queen St. CT6 33 B3
Queens Gdns. CT6 33 C3
Ravensbourne Av. CT6 33 D5
Reynolds Clo. CT6 33 D4
Richmond St. CT6 33 B3
Roselea Av. CT6 33 C5
St Andrews Clo. CT6 33 C4
St Annes Dri. CT6 33 A4
St Georges Ter. CT6 33 A3
Sandown Dri. CT6 33 A4
Sea St. CT6 33 A4
Sea View Sq. CT6 33 B3
South Rd. CT6 33 C4
Southsea Dri. CT6 33 A4
Spenser Rd. CT6 33 B4
Stanley Gdns. CT6 33 C4
Stanley Rd. CT6 33 C4
Station Chine. CT6 33 B4
Station Rd. CT6 33 B3
Swale Clo. CT6 33 D5
Telford St. CT6 33 B3
Thanet Way. CT6 33 A5
The Broadway. CT6 33 A3
The Circus. CT6 33 A4
The Downings. CT6 34 D5
Thunderland Rd. CT6 33 B3
Tower Gdns. CT6 33 B3
Tyndal Park. CT6 33 D4
Underdown La. CT6 33 C5
Underdown Rd. CT6 33 C5
Victoria Park. CT6 33 C3
Western Av. CT6 33 A4
Western Esp. CT6 33 A3
William St. CT6 33 B3
York Clo. CT6 33 A4
York Rd. CT6 33 A3

HYTHE

Albert La. CT21 35 A5
Albert Rd. CT21 35 A5
Albion Pl. CT21 35 C4
Arthur Rd. CT21 35 A5
Bank St. CT21 35 A4
Bartholomew St. CT21 35 A4
Basset Av. CT21 35 C2
Basset Gdns. CT21 35 C2
Beaconsfield Ter. CT21 35 C5
Bell Inn Rd. CT21 35 A4
Blackhouse Hill. CT21 35 C3
Blackhouse Rise. CT21 35 C3
Cannongate Av. CT21 35 C3
Cannongate Clo. CT21 35 B3
Cannongate Gdns. CT21 35 C3
Cannongate Rd. CT21 35 C3
Castle Av. CT21 35 A3
Castle Cres. CT21 35 A2
Castle Rd. CT21 35 A1
Chapel St. CT21 35 A4
Church Hill. CT21 35 A4
Church Rd. CT21 35 B4
Cinque Ports Av. CT21 35 A5
Claridge Mews. CT21 35 A4
Cliff Clo. CT21 35 C3
Cliff Rd. CT21 35 C2
Coastguard Cotts. CT21 35 A6
Cobay Clo. CT21 35 B4
Cobbs Pass. CT21 35 B4
Cobden Rd. CT21 35 A6
Deedes Clo. CT21 35 B3
Dental St. CT21 35 B4
Douglas Av. CT21 35 B4
Earlsfield Rd. CT21 35 B4
East St. CT21 35 B4
Elizabeth Gdns. CT21 35 A5
Elm Gdns. CT21 35 A5
Farmer Clo. CT21 35 C2
Fisher Clo. CT21 35 C5
Foys Pass. CT21 35 B4
Grange Rd. CT21 35 A1
Great Conduit St. CT21 35 A4
Hafod Pass. CT21 35 B4
High St. CT21 35 A4
Hillcrest Rd. CT21 35 A3
Hillside St. CT21 35 A4
Kings Head La. CT21 35 B4
Ladies Walk. CT21 35 B5
Lookers La. CT21 35 A2
Lower Blackhouse Hill. CT21 35 C3
Lucys Hill. CT21 35 A4
Lucys Walk. CT21 35 B5

Lynton Rd. CT21 35 A5
Malthouse Hill. CT21 35 A4
Marine Par. CT21 35 B6
Marine Walk St. CT21 35 B4
Market Hill. CT21 35 A4
Mill La. CT21 35 C4
Mill Rd. CT21 35 B4
Mount St. CT21 35 A4
Moyle Tower Rd. CT21 35 B6
Napier Gdns. CT21 35 A5
New Prospect Rd. CT21 35 A4
New Rd. CT21 35 A5
Newington Mdw. CT21 35 C3
North Rd. CT21 35 A4
Oak Hall Pass. CT21 35 A4
Oak Walk. CT21 35 A4
Orchard Dri. CT21 35 A5
Ormonde Rd. CT21 35 A5
Park Rd. CT21 35 A5
Portland Rd. CT21 35 A5
Princes Par. CT21 35 C5
Prospect Rd. CT21 35 B4
Quarry Clo. CT21 35 A3
Quarry La. CT21 35 A3
Queens Ct. CT21 35 A5
Red Lion Ct. CT21 35 A4
St Hildas Rd. CT21 35 A6
St Leonards Ct. CT21 35 A5
St Leonards Rd. CT21 35 A5
Saxon Clo. CT21 35 D4
School Rd. CT21 35 A2
Seabrook Rd. CT21 35 C4
Seaton Av. CT21 35 A3
Sene Park. CT21 35 C3
South Rd. CT21 35 B5
Stade St. CT21 35 A5
Station Rd. CT21 35 B4
Sturdy Clo. CT21 35 A5
Sun La. CT21 35 B4
Tanners Hill. CT21 35 A2
Tanners Hill Gdns. CT21 35 A2
The Avenue. CT21 35 B4
The Close. CT21 35 A4
The Dene. CT21 35 B4
The Fairway. CT21 35 B5
Theatre St. CT21 35 B4
Theresa Rd. CT21 35 A6
Tower Gdns. CT21 35 B4
Twiss Av. CT21 35 B4
Twiss Gro. CT21 35 C4
Twiss Rd. CT21 35 C4
Upper Malthouse Hill. CT21 35 A4
Victoria Rd. CT21 35 A5
Wakefield Walk. CT21 35 B5
West Par. CT21 35 A6
William Pitt Clo. CT21 35 B4
Windmill St. CT21 35 A5
Wood Rd. CT21 35 A5

LENHAM

Ashford Rd. ME17 34 C5
Atwater Ct. ME17 34 C5
Beacon Rd. ME17 34 B5
Cherry Clo. ME17 34 B5
Chilston Rd. ME17 34 C5
Church Sq. ME17 34 C5
Croft Gdns. ME17 34 B5
Douglas Rd. ME17 34 C5
Faversham Rd. ME17 34 C4
Foord Rd. ME17 34 B4
Frogmore Walk. ME17 34 A4
Glebe Gdns. ME17 34 C5
Grovelands. ME17 34 C5
Ham La. ME17 34 A5
Hatch Rd. ME17 34 B5
Headcorn Rd. ME17 34 B5
High St. ME17 34 B5
Honywood Rd. ME17 34 A5
INDUSTRIAL ESTATES:
Lenham Storage Freightflow Depot. ME17 34 A5
Lenham By-Pass. ME17 34 B4
Loder Clo. ME17 34 A5
Maidstone Rd. ME17 34 A4
Mill Clo. ME17 34 B6
Mitchell Clo. ME17 34 B5
Morella Walk. ME17 34 A5
Napoleon Walk. ME17 34 A5
Old Ham La. ME17 34 A5
Old School Clo. ME17 34 B5
Rivers Walk. ME17 34 B5

Robins Av. ME17 34 B5
Robins Clo. ME17 34 B5
Royton Av. ME17 34 C4
Swadelands Clo. ME17 34 B4
The Cloisters. ME17 34 A4
The Square. ME17 34 C5
Wickham Pl. ME17 34 C5

LYDD

Ash Gro. TN29 36 D1
Bleak Rd. TN29 36 B2
Brooks Way. TN29 36 C3
Cannon St. TN29 36 C2
Church Rd. TN29 36 C2
Colemans Clo. TN29 36 C2
Copperfields. TN29 36 B2
Dengemarsh Rd. TN29 36 C3
Dennes La. TN29 36 B1
Dungeness Rd. TN29 36 C2
Eastern Rd. TN29 36 C2
George Wood Clo. TN29 36 C2
Gillett Rd. TN29 36 D1
Green Way. TN29 36 B3
Grisbrook Farm Clo. TN29 36 C2
Harden Rd. TN29 36 C2
High St. TN29 36 B3
Jaarlen Rd. TN29 36 B3
Jurys Gap Rd. TN29 36 A3
Kitewell La. TN29 36 D1
Manor Rd. TN29 36 C3
Mill Rd. TN29 36 C2
Ness Rd. TN29 36 C2
New La. TN29 36 B2
New St. TN29 36 C2
Oak La. TN29 36 B2
Park St. TN29 36 B3
Poplar La. TN29 36 C2
Queens Rd. TN29 36 B2
Queens Way. TN29 36 B2
Robin Hood La. TN29 36 C3
Rype Clo. TN29 36 B3
Skinner Rd. TN29 36 C2
South St. TN29 36 C2
Station Rd. TN29 36 C2
Sycamore Clo. TN29 36 C1
The Derings. TN29 36 B2
The Green. TN29 36 B3
Tourney Rd. TN29 36 B3
Vinelands. TN29 36 B2

MAIDSTONE

Aden Ter. ME14 37 A1
Albany St. ME14 37 C3
Albert St. ME14 37 A2
Albion Pl. ME14 37 B4
Aldon Clo. ME14 37 D2
Alexandra St. ME14 37 A3
Alkham Rd. ME14 37 D4
Allen St. ME14 37 B3
Andrew Broughton Way. ME14 37 C4
Ardenlee Dri. ME14 37 C3
Arlott Clo. ME14 37 A2
Arundel St. ME14 37 A2
Ashford Rd. ME14 37 C4
Ashurst Rd. ME14 37 D3
Astley St. ME14 37 B4
Bank St. ME14 37 A5
Bannister Rd. ME14 37 B1
Barbados Ter. ME14 37 B1
Barden Ct. ME14 37 G3
Bargrove Rd. ME14 37 D2
Barker Rd. ME16 37 A5
Barton Rd. ME15 37 B6
Basing Clo. ME15 37 B6
Basmere Clo. ME14 37 D2
Bearsted Rd. ME14 37 D2
Bedgebury Clo. ME14 37 D3
Birch Tree Way. ME15 37 C6
Birchington Clo. ME14 37 D4
Bishopsway. ME15 37 A5
Blean Sq. ME14 37 D2
Blendon Rd. ME14 37 D3
Bloomsbury Wk. ME14 37 B4
Bluett St. ME14 37 B3
Blythe Rd. ME15 37 C5
Bonnington Rd. ME14 37 D2
Boxley Clo. ME14 37 C1
Boxley Rd. ME14 37 B3
Brackley Clo. ME14 37 C3
Bredgar Clo. ME14 37 C3
Brewer St. ME14 37 B4
Broadway. ME14 37 A5
Brooks Pl. ME14 37 B4
Brunswick St. ME15 37 B5
Brunswick St East. ME15 37 B5
Bychurch Pl. ME15 37 B6
Byron Rd. ME14 37 C1
Calder Rd. ME14 37 A1
Calehill Clo. ME14 37 D2
Camden St. ME14 37 B3
Campbell Rd. ME15 37 B6
Canada Ter. ME14 37 B1
Canning St. ME14 37 B2
Challock Walk. ME14 37 D2
Chancery La. ME15 37 B5
Chatham Rd. ME14 37 A1
Chattenden Ct. ME14 37 C2
Chillington St. ME14 37 A2
Church St. ME14 37 B4
Claremont Rd. ME14 37 C3
Clifton Clo. ME14 37 C3
College Av. ME15 37 A6
College Rd. ME15 37 A6
College Walk. ME15 37 B6
Command Rd. ME14 37 A1
Commodore Rd. ME14 37 C3
Consort Clo. ME14 37 C4
Cooling Clo. ME14 37 D2
Corrall Ct. ME14 37 C4
County Rd. ME14 37 A3
Cowden Rd. ME14 37 D3
Crayford Clo. ME14 37 D3
Cromwell Rd. ME14 37 B4
Cross St. ME14 37 B2
Cudham Clo. ME14 37 D3
Curzon Rd. ME14 37 B2
Cutbush Ct. ME14 37 C4
Dickens Rd. ME14 37 A1
Dhekelia Clo. ME14 37 A1
Dixon Clo. ME14 37 A6
Dunera Dri. ME14 37 B1
Earl St. ME14 37 A4
Eastwell Clo. ME14 37 D3
Eccleston Rd. ME15 37 A6
Elm Gro. ME15 37 C5
Fairmeadow. ME14 37 A4
Faraday Rd. ME14 37 C1
Farningham Clo. ME14 37 D2
Fiji Ter. ME14 37 B1
Fintonagh Dri. ME14 37 C2
Fisher St. ME14 37 B2
Flower Rise. ME14 37 A2
Foley St. ME14 37 B3
Foster St. ME15 37 B5
*Friars Ct, Queen Anne Rd. ME14 37 B4
Gabriels Hill. ME15 37 B4
Garrington Clo. ME14 37 D2
George St. ME15 37 B6
Gladstone Rd. ME14 37 B2
Goldthorne Clo. ME14 37 C4
Granville Rd. ME14 37 B2
Grapple Rd. ME14 37 A1
Grecian St. ME14 37 B2
Green Side. ME14 37 C5
Guston Rd. ME14 37 D3
Hadlow Rd. ME14 37 D3
Hampton Rd. ME14 37 D2
Hardy St. ME14 37 B3
Hart St. ME14 37 A6
Hastings Rd. ME15 37 B5
Hatherall Rd. ME14 37 C2
Havock La. ME14 37 A4
Hayle Rd. ME15 37 B6
Heathfield Av. ME14 37 D1
Heathfield Clo. ME14 37 C1
Heathfield Rd. ME14 37 C1
Heathorn St. ME14 37 B3
Hedley St. ME14 37 B3
Hengist Ct. ME14 37 B4
High St. ME14 37 A5
Hillary Rd. ME14 37 B2
Holland Rd. ME14 37 B3
Holm Oaks. ME14 37 D3
Honduras Ter. ME14 37 B1
Hope St. ME14 37 A3
Huntsman La. ME14 37 C4
INDUSTRIAL ESTATES:
Hart St Commercial Centre. ME16 37 A5
St Peter St Ind Centre. ME16 37 A4
Invicta Park. ME14 37 A1
Jamaica Ter. ME14 37 B1
James St. ME14 37 B3
James Whatman Way. ME14 37 A3
Jeffrey St. ME14 37 B4
John St. ME14 37 B2
Kenya Ter. ME14 37 B2
Kewlands. ME14 37 D2
King Edward Rd. ME15 37 A6
King St. ME14 37 B4
Kingsley Rd. ME15 37 B5
Knightrider St. ME15 37 B5
Knott Ct. ME14 37 A2
Knowle Rd. ME14 37 B2
Langton Clo. ME14 37 D4
Lenfield Av. ME14 37 C4
Libya Ter. ME14 37 B2
Littlebourne Rd. ME14 37 D2
Lombardy Dri. ME14 37 D3
Lower Boxley Rd. ME14 37 A3
Lower Rd. ME15 37 C6
Lower Stone St. ME15 37 B5
Lucerne St. ME14 37 B3
Luddenham Clo. ME14 37 D2
Malta Ter. ME14 37 B2
Market Blds. ME14 37 A4
Market St. ME14 37 A4
Marsham St. ME14 37 B4
Marston Dri. ME14 37 C4
Matfield Cres. ME14 37 C3
Meadow Walk. ME15 37 C5
Medway St. ME14 37 A4
Melville Rd. ME15 37 B5
Middle Row. ME14 37 A4
Mill St. ME15 37 A5
Milstead Clo. ME14 37 D4
Moncktons La. ME14 37 A2
Mostyn Rd. ME14 37 D4
Mote Av. ME15 37 C5
Mote Rd. ME15 37 B5
Muir Rd. ME15 37 B6
Museum St. ME14 37 A4
Newington Wk. ME14 37 D2
*Newlyn Ct, Wyatt St. ME14 37 B4
Norman Clo. ME14 37 C2
North Way. ME14 37 C1
Northdown Clo. ME14 37 C1
Northfleet Clo. ME14 37 D3
Norway Ter. ME14 37 A2
Old Tovil Rd. ME15 37 A6
Orchard St. ME15 37 B6
Pads Hill. ME15 37 B5
Padsole La. ME15 37 B5
Palace Av. ME15 37 A5
Park Av. ME14 37 C2
Peel St. ME14 37 B2
Penenden Heath Rd. ME14 37 C1
Penenden St. ME14 37 B3
Perry St. ME14 37 A2
Perryfield St. ME14 37 A3
Pine Gro. ME14 37 C2
Plaistow Sq. ME14 37 D2
Princes St. ME14 37 B3
Priory Rd. ME15 37 B5
Pudding La. ME14 37 A4
Quarry Sq. ME14 37 B3
Queen Anne Rd. ME14 37 B4
Randall St. ME14 37 A3
Rawdon Rd. ME15 37 B6
Recreation Clo. ME14 37 C3
Redcliffe La. ME14 37 B2
River View. ME15 37 A6
Rock Rd. ME14 37 B2
Roman Heights. ME14 37 C2
Romney Pl. ME15 37 B5
Rose Yard. ME14 37 A4
Royal Engineers Rd. ME14 37 A1
*Royal Star Arcade, High St. ME14 37 A5
St Faiths St. ME14 37 A4
St Lukes Av. ME14 37 C3
St Lukes Rd. ME14 37 C3
St Peter St. ME16 37 A4
St Philips Av. ME15 37 C6
Salem St. ME15 37 B6
Salisbury Rd. ME14 37 B2
Sandling La. ME14 37 B1
Sandling Rd. ME14 37 A2
Sandy La. ME14 37 D1
Saxons Dri. ME14 37 C2
Scott St. ME14 37 A3
Sessions House Sq. ME14 37 A3
Sheals Cres. ME15 37 B6
Sittingbourne Rd. ME14 37 C4
Snowdon Av. ME14 37 C4
Spearhead Rd. ME14 37 A1
Spindle Glade. ME14 37 D3
Sportsfield. ME14 37 C3
Square Hill. ME15 37 C4
Square Hill Rd. ME15 37 C5
Staceys St. ME14 37 A3
Starnes Ct. ME14 37 B4
Station Rd. ME14 37 A4
Stuart Clo. ME14 37 C2
Sunningdale Ct. ME14 37 C4
Terry Yard. ME14 37 B4
The Hedges. ME14 37 B1
Thornhill Pl. ME14 37 B2
Tudor Av. ME14 37 C2
Tufton St. ME14 37 B4
Turkey Ct. ME15 37 D5
Underwood Clo. ME15 37 A6
Union St. ME14 37 B4
Upper Rd. ME15 37 C6
Upper Stone St. ME15 37 B5
Vinters Rd. ME14 37 C4
Wat Tyler Way. ME15 37 B5
Waterloo St. ME15 37 B6
Waterlow Rd. ME14 37 B3
Waters Edge. ME15 37 A6
Waterside. ME14 37 A4
Week St. ME14 37 A4
Well Rd. ME14 37 B3
Wellington Pl. ME14 37 A2
West Park Rd. ME15 37 C6
Weyhill Clo. ME14 37 D2
Whatman Clo. ME14 37 D2
Wheeler St. ME14 37 B4
Wheeler St Hedges. ME14 37 C2
Willow Way. ME15 37 C6
Winchester House. ME14 37 B3
Windsor Clo. ME14 37 C3
Woodland Way. ME14 37 C1
Woodlands Clo. ME14 37 B1
Woodville Rd. ME15 37 B6
Woollett St. ME14 37 B3
Wordsworth Rd. ME14 37 C1
Wyatt St. ME14 37 B4
Wyke Manor Rd. ME14 37 B4

MARDEN

Albion Rd. TN12 36 C5
Allens. TN12 36 C5
Ballard Clo. TN12 36 B5
Barnes Wk. TN12 36 C5
Barrel Arch Clo. TN12 36 A5
Bramley Ct. TN12 36 A5
Chantry Pl. TN12 36 B5
Chantry Rd. TN12 36 B5
Church Grn. TN12 36 B5
Copper La. TN12 36 C6
Cranham Sq. TN12 36 B5
Crest. TN12 36 B4
Goudhurst Rd. TN12 36 A6
Haffenden Clo. TN12 36 B5
High St. TN12 36 B5
Howland Rd. TN12 36 C5
INDUSTRIAL ESTATES:
Guardian Ind Est. TN12 36 A4
Jewell Gro. TN12 36 C5
Lime Clo. TN12 36 B5
Lucks Way. TN12 36 A5
Maidstone Rd. TN12 36 C5
Maynards. TN12 36 B5
Meades Clo. TN12 36 A5
Meadow Way. TN12 36 C5
Merchant Pl. TN12 36 B5
Napoleon Dri. TN12 36 B5
Oak Tree Clo. TN12 36 C5
Pattenden La. TN12 36 A4
Plain Rd. TN12 36 C6
Plantation La. TN12 36 A5
Roundel Way. TN12 30 B5
South Rd. TN12 36 C5
Sovereigns Way. TN12 36 A5
Stanley Rd. TN12 36 C5
Stella Clo. TN12 36 B5
Sunburst Clo. TN12 36 B5
Sutton Ct. TN12 36 B5
Sutton Forge. TN12 36 B5
The Cockpit. TN12 36 B5
Thorn Rd. TN12 36 C6
West End. TN12 36 B5

MARGATE

Addington Rd. CT9 38
Addington Sq. CT9 38
Addington St. CT9 38
Addiscombe Gdns. CT9 38 D
Addiscombe Rd. CT9 38 D
Albert Rd. CT9 38 E
Albert Ter. CT9 38 C
Alexandra Homes. CT9 38 C
Alexandra Rd. CT9 38 C
Alexandra Ter. CT9 38 C
Alkali Row. CT9 38 C
All Saints Av. CT9 38 A
Alma Rd. CT9 38 D
Argyle Av. CT9 38 A
Argyle Gdns. CT9 38 A
Arnold Rd. CT9 38 D
Athelstan Rd. CT9 38 D
Bath Pl. CT9 38 D
Bath Rd. CT9 38 D
Beatrice Rd. CT9 38 C
Belgrave Rd. CT9 38 C
Bilton Sq. CT9 38 C
Booth Pl. CT9 38 D
Broad St. CT9 38 C
Brockley Rd. CT9 38 D
Buckingham Rd. CT9 38 C
Buenos Ayres. CT9 38 E
Burlington Gdns. CT9 38 A
Byron Av. CT9 38 D
Canterbury Rd. CT9 38 A
Caroline Sq. CT9 38 D
Carlisle Sq. CT9 38 D
Carroways Pl. CT9 38 D
Caxton Rd. CT9 38 A
Cecil Sq. CT9 38 C
Cecil St. CT9 38 C
Chapel Hill Clo. CT9 38 D
Charlotte Sq. CT9 38 C
Church Rd. CT9 38 D
Church St. CT9 38 D
Churchfields. CT9 38 C
Churchfields Pl. CT9 38 C
Cliff Ter. CT9 38 D
Clifton Gdns. CT9 38 D
Clifton Pl. CT9 38 D
Clifton Rd. CT9 38 D
Clifton St. CT9 38 D
Cobbs Pl. CT9 38 C
College Rd. CT9 38 C
College Walk. CT9 38 C
Connaught Gdns. CT9 38 D
Connaught Rd. CT9 38 D
Cowper Rd. CT9 38 D
Craven Clo. CT9 38 A
Crescent Rd. CT9 38 E
Dalby Rd. CT9 38 D
Dalby Sq. CT9 38 D
Dane Hill. CT9 38 D
Dane Hill Row. CT9 38 D
Dane Park Rd. CT9 38 D
Dane Rd. CT9 38 D
Danesmead Ter. CT9 38 D
Dene Walk. CT9 38 D
Drapers Av. CT9 38 D
Duke St. CT9 38 C
Durban Rd. CT9 38 D
Eaton Hill. CT9 38 C
Eaton Rd. CT9 38 C
Elmley Way. CT9 38 D
Empire Ter. CT9 38 C
Ethelbert Gdns. CT9 38 D
Ethelbert Rd. CT9 38 D
Ethelbert Ter. CT9 38 D
Farley Rd. CT9 38 D
Firbank Gdns. CT9 38 B
Fort Cres. CT9 38 D
Fort Hill. CT9 38 C
Fort Prom. CT9 38 C
Fort Rd. CT9 38 C
Fulham Av. CT9 38 A
Fulsam Pl. CT9 38 B
Garfield Rd. CT9 38 E
George V Av. CT9 38 A
Giles Gdns. CT9 38 D
Gladstone Rd. CT9 38 C
Grosvenor Gdns. CT9 38 C
Grosvenor Hill. CT9 38 C
Grosvenor Pl. CT9 38 C
Grotto Gdns. CT9 38 D
Grotto Hill. CT9 38 D
Grotto Rd. CT9 38 D

rove Gdns. CT9	38 A3	Wellis Gdns. CT9	38 A3
alfmile Ride. CT9	38 C6	Westbrook Av. CT9	38 A3
artsdown Rd. CT9	38 A3	Westbrook Cotts. CT9	38 A3
atfield Rd. CT9	38 A3	Westbrook Gdns. CT9	38 A3
awley Sq. CT9	38 C2	Westbrook Prom. CT9	38 A3
awley St. CT9	38 C2	Westbrook Rd. CT9	38 A3
eather Clo. CT9	38 A4	Westcliff Gdns. CT9	38 A3
elena Av. CT9	38 C4	Westcliff Rd. CT9	38 A3
gh St. CT9	38 C2	Westfield Rd. CT9	38 A4
ghfield Gdns. CT9	38 A3	Willow Way. CT9	38 A4
oneysuckle Clo. CT9	38 A4	Yoakley Sq. CT9	38 D4

INDUSTRIAL ESTATES:
Tivoli Ind Est. CT9 38 C3
Westwood Ind Est. CT9 38 D6
acob Clo. CT9 38 B5
ng St. CT9 38 C2
ngston Av. CT9 38 A5
nold Park. CT9 38 B5
ausanne Rd. CT9 38 C2
avender Clo. CT9 38 A4
ster Rd. CT9 38 D4
ombard St. CT9 38 C2
ove La. CT9 38 C2
anston Rd. CT9 38 B6
arine Dri. CT9 38 C2
arine Gdns. CT9 38 C2
arine Ter. CT9 38 B2
arket St. CT9 38 C2
arlborough Rd. CT9 38 C3
ere Gate. CT9 38 C4
ill La. CT9 38 C3
ilton Av. CT9 38 D3
ash Court Gdns. CT9 38 C4
ash Court Rd. CT9 38 D5
ash La. CT9 38 D5
ash Rd. CT9 38 C5
aylands. CT9 38 A3
ew Cross St. CT9 38 C2
ew St. CT9 38 C2
orthdown Rd. CT9 38 C2
ast CT. CT9 38 D4
ld School Gdns. CT9 38 D4
sborne Ter. CT9 38 D3
xford St. CT9 38 D3
ark Cres Rd. CT9 38 D3
ark La. CT9 38 D2
ark Pl. CT9 38 C3
ark Rd. CT9 38 D3
ayton Clo. CT9 38 D6
erkins Av. CT9 38 D4
ets Corner. CT9 38 C3
incess Cres. CT9 38 C3
inces St. CT9 38 C2
ailway Ter. CT9 38 B3
amsgate Rd. CT9 38 A3
ancorn Rd. CT9 38 A3
owe Clo. CT9 38 D5
oyal Cres. CT9 38 B3
oyal Esp. CT9 38 A3
Andrews Clo. CT9 38 D5
Annes Gdns. CT9 38 D5
Augustines Av. CT9 38 C4
Johns Rd. CT9 38 C3
Johns St. CT9 38 C3
Peters Ftpth. CT9 38 D3
Peters Rd. CT9 38 D3
almestone Rd. CT9 38 C4
anger Clo. CT9 38 G4
ea View Ter. CT9 38 A3
etterfield Rd. CT9 38 D3
hakespeare Pass. CT9 38 B3
hakespeare Rd. CT9 38 B3
hottendane Rd. CT9 38 D3
ation Rd. CT9 38 B3
ussex Av. CT9 38 D3
wallow Clo. CT9 38 A4
ycamore Clo. CT9 38 B5
hor Rd. CT9 38 D2
he Avenue. CT9 38 D3
he Parade. CT9 38 C2
he Rendezvous. CT9 38 C1
voli Brook. CT9 38 C3
voli Park Av. CT9 38 B3
nity Pl. CT9 38 C2
nity Sq. CT9 38 C1
ster Rd. CT9 38 C4
nion Cres. CT9 38 C2
nion Row. CT9 38 C2
pper Gro. CT9 38 D2
carage Cres. CT9 38 C3
carage Pl. CT9 38 C3
ctoria Rd. CT9 38 C3
alpole Rd. CT9 38 D2
averley Rd. CT9 38 A4

Westcliff Rd. CT9 38 A3
Zion Pl. CT9 38 D2

MINSTER

Abbey Clo. ME12 39 C4
Abbeyview Dri. ME12 39 A3
Alaseun Ter. ME12 39 A3
Alston Clo. ME12 39 A3
Augustine Rd. ME12 39 A1
Back La. ME12 39 C3
Baldwin Rd. ME12 39 C3
Barton Hill Dri. ME12 39 A5
Bellvue Rd. ME12 39 B3
Blatcher Clo. ME12 39 B4
Boundary Clo. ME12 39 D4
Bramston Rd. ME12 39 C4
Brecon Chase. ME12 39 B3
Chapel St. ME12 39 C3
Chiddingfold Clo. ME12 39 C4
Churchill Rd. ME12 39 D3
Cliff Gdns. ME12 39 D3
Clovelly Dri. ME12 39 A2
Copland Av. ME12 39 B4
Darlington Dri. ME12 39 C4
Drake Av. ME12 39 C4
Dreadnought Av. ME12 39 A4
Echo Wk. ME12 39 D4
Edwina Av. ME12 39 A3
Elm La. ME12 39 C5
Emley Rd. ME12 39 C4
Falcon Gdns. ME12 39 C3
Fleetwood Clo. ME12 39 A4
Forty Acres Hill. ME12 39 B6
Glendale Rd. ME12 39 A3
Glenwood Dri. ME12 39 B3
Greyhound Dri. ME12 39 B4
Harps Av. ME12 39 B4
Harps Walk. ME12 39 B4
High St. ME12 39 C3
Highview Rd. ME12 39 C3
Hillside Rd. ME12 39 A3
Hopsons Pl. ME12 39 C4
Howard Clo. ME12 39 B2
Imperial Av. ME12 39 C3
Johnson Way. ME12 39 A3
Kent Av. ME12 39 A3
Kings Rd. ME12 39 C3
Love La. ME12 39 C3
Lower Rd. ME12 39 A6
Lynmouth Dri. ME12 39 C3
Magpie Clo. ME12 39 A4
Mallard Ct. ME12 39 A4
Marina Dri. ME12 39 A3
Mill Hill. ME12 39 C3
Minster Dri. ME12 39 B2
Minster Rd. ME12 39 C3
Nautilus Clo. ME12 39 B2
Nautilus Dri. ME12 39 C3
Nelson Av. ME12 39 C4
New Rd. ME12 39 B4
Noreen Av. ME12 39 A3
Norwood Rise. ME12 39 B3
Ocean Ter. ME12 39 D3
Orchard Gro. ME12 39 B4
Parish Rd. ME12 39 A5
Petfield Clo. ME12 39 C4
Porter Clo. ME12 39 A4
Prince Charles Av. ME12 39 C4
Princes Av. ME12 39 C3
Queenborough Dri. ME12 39 A3
Queens Rd. ME12 39 C3
Rodmer Clo. ME12 39 B2
Saxon Av. ME12 39 A3
Scoles Rd. ME12 39 A3
Scarborough Dri. ME12 39 A1
Scrapsgate Rd. ME12 39 A3
Sea Side Av. ME12 39 B2
Seathorpe Av. ME12 39 A3
Sexburga Dri. ME12 39 A1
Shurland Av. ME12 39 A3

Southsea Av. ME12 39 A1
Stanley Av. ME12 39 C3
Sunnyside Av. ME12 39 A4
Tams Gdns. ME12 39 D4
The Broadway. ME12 39 A2
The Glen. ME12 39 A2
The Leas. ME12 39 B1
The Maples. ME12 39 A3
The Rowans. ME12 39 A3
Union Rd. ME12 39 C3
Vicarage Rd. ME12 39 C3
Wards Hill Rd. ME12 39 A2
Waterloo Hill. ME12 39 C3
Waverley Av. ME12 39 A3
Westcliff Dri. ME12 39 C2
Whitethorne Gdns. ME12 39 D3
Whybornes Chase. ME12 39 B4
Windmill Rise. ME12 39 C3
Woodland Dri. ME12 39 A2
Worcester Clo. ME12 39 B4

NEW ROMNEY

Anne Roper Clo. TN28 40 E3
Armada Clo. TN28 40 F4
Ashdown Cres. TN28 40 D4
Ashford Rd. TN28 40 A2
Blenheim Rd. TN28 40 E3
Brissenden Clo. TN28 40 C2
Broadlands Av. TN28 40 C1
Broadlands Cres. TN28 40 C1
Cannon St. TN28 40 D1
Carey Clo. TN28 40 C2
Cherry Gdns. TN28 40 E3
Church App. TN28 40 B3
Church La. TN28 40 B3
Church Rd. TN28 40 B3
Clarendon Mews. TN28 40 D1
Coast Rd. TN28 40 F3
Cockreed La. TN28 40 B2
Craythorne Clo. TN28 40 C1
Craythorne Rd. TN28 40 C1
Daglish Clo. TN28 40 C3
Darcy Sq. TN28 40 E4
Dymchurch Rd. TN28 40 D1
Ellesmere Mews. TN28 40 D1
Ellis Dri. TN28 40 C1
Fairfield Clo. TN28 40 B3
Fairfield Rd. TN28 40 B3
George La. TN28 40 C3
Gloucester Mws. TN28 40 D1
Grand Par. TN28 40 F3
Greenly Way. TN28 40 F4
Hardwick Dri. TN28 40 C1
Haywards Clo. TN28 40 C3
High St. TN28 40 D3
Imbert Clo. TN28 40 D3
Langport Rd. TN28 40 C2
Learoyd Rd. TN28 40 C3
Links Way. TN28 40 E3
Lions Rd. TN28 40 D3
Littlestone Rd. TN28 40 D3
Lydd Rd. TN28 40 A3
Mabledon Clo. TN28 40 C3
Madeira Rd. TN28 40 F3
Marine Par. TN28 40 E3
Marlborough Clo. TN28 40 E3
Marsh Cres. TN28 40 C3
Melbury Mews. TN28 40 C1
Mountfield Rd. TN28 40 D3
Nether Av. TN28 40 E3
North St. TN28 40 B3
Oak Lodge Rd. TN28 40 C2
Park Rd. TN28 40 B3
Pembroke Mews. TN28 40 C1
Priory Clo. TN28 40 A3
Queens Rd. TN28 40 B3
Richmond Dri. TN28 40 E3
Rolfe La. TN28 40 B3
Rome Rd. TN28 40 B3
Ryswick Mews. TN28 40 C1
St Andrews Rd. TN28 40 C3
St Johns St. TN28 40 C3
St Martins Rd. TN28 40 B3
St Marys Rd. TN28 40 C3
St Nicholas Rd. TN28 40 D3
Spitalfield St. TN28 40 D3
Springwood Ct. TN28 40 D3
Station App. TN28 40 D3
Station Rd. TN28 40 D3
Sussex Rd. TN28 40 A3
The Churchlands. TN28 40 D3
The Fairway. TN28 40 E3

The Saltings. TN28 40 F4
Tookey Rd. TN28 40 B3
Tritton La. TN28 40 B3
Victoria Rd. TN28 40 F4
Victoria Rd West. TN28 40 E4
Victoria St. TN28 40 B3
Walner Gdns. TN28 40 C2
Walner La. TN28 40 C2
Warren Rd. TN28 40 D3
Wells Clo. TN28 40 D3
West St. TN28 40 B3
Wiles Av. TN28 40 C3
Windsor Mews. TN28 40 C2

NORTHFLEET

Aspdin Rd. DA11 41 D6
Bankside. DA11 41 B2
Buckingham Rd. DA11 41 D3
Burnaby Rd. DA11 41 D3
Camden Clo. DA11 41 C4
Chadwick Clo. DA11 41 D4
Chaucer Rd. DA11 41 C6
Chiffinch Gdns. DA11 41 D6
Chiltern Rd. DA11 41 D6
Church Walk. DA11 41 B2
Coldharbour Rd. DA11 41 D5
College Rd. DA11 41 A1
Colyer Rd. DA11 41 C5
Constable Rd. DA11 41 D6
Cotswolds Rd. DA11 41 D6
Coulton Av. DA11 41 D4
Council Av. DA11 41 B2
Crete Hall Rd. DA11 41 C2
Danes Clo. DA11 41 B6
Davis Av. DA11 41 D4
Dene Holm Rd. DA11 41 C6
Detling Rd. DA11 41 D6
Dover Rd. DA11 41 B3
Dudley Rd. DA11 41 D3
Eagle Way. DA11 41 A1
Earl Rd. DA11 41 D5
East Kent Av. DA11 41 B2
Ebbsfleet Walk. DA11 41 A2
Factory Rd. DA11 41 D6
Falcon Mews. DA11 41 D5
First Av. DA11 41 D4
Fishermans Hill. DA11 41 B1
Fleet Rd. DA11 41 B6
Ford Rd. DA11 41 B1
Fortrye Clo. DA11 41 D5
Gainsborough Dri. DA11 41 C6
Gordon Rd. DA11 41 D3
Gouge Av. DA11 41 D4
Granby Rd. DA11 41 C2
Greendale Walk. DA11 41 A1
Grove Rd. DA11 41 A1
Gwynn Rd. DA11 41 C1
Haldane Gdns. DA11 41 C4
Hall Rd. DA11 41 B6
Hamerton Rd. DA11 41 A1
Harrowby Gdns. DA11 41 D5
Hartfield Pl. DA11 41 C3
Hatton Clo. DA11 41 D3
High St. DA11 41 B2
Hillary Av. DA11 41 C3
Hive La. DA11 41 C3
Hog La. DA11 41 C3
Huntley Av. DA11 41 B2
INDUSTRIAL ESTATES:
Springhead Enterprise Park. DA11 41 B4
Johnson Clo. DA11 41 B2
Kingston Ct. DA11 41 B2
Laburnam Gro. DA11 41 C3
Landseer Av. DA11 41 D6
Langdale Walk. DA11 41 A1
Larkfields. DA11 41 C5
Lawn Rd. DA11 41 B1
Lime Av. DA11 41 C3
London Rd. DA11 41 A1
Lower Rd. DA11 41 A1
Marconi Rd. DA11 41 C1
Masefield Rd. DA11 41 C3
Meadow Rd. DA11 41 C5
Mill Rd. DA11 41 D3
Millfield Dri. DA11 41 D5
Mitchell Av. DA11 41 C6
Mulberry Rd. DA11 41 D6
New Barn Rd. DA13 41 B4
North Kent Av. DA11 41 B2
Old Perry St. DA11 41 B1
Orchard Rd. DA11 41 C3
Painters Ash La. DA11 41 C6

Park Av. DA11 41 D4
Pennine Way. DA11 41 D6
Pepper Hill. DA11 41 B6
Pepper Hill La. DA11 41 B6
Pepys Clo. DA11 41 C6
Pickwick Gdns. DA11 41 C6
Plane Av. DA11 41 D3
Portland Rd. DA12 41 C2
Preston Rd. DA11 41 D4
Railway St. DA11 41 A1
Rembrandt Dri. DA11 41 D6
Riversdale. DA11 41 D6
Robinia Av. DA11 41 C3
Roman Rd. DA11 41 C6
Romney Rd. DA11 41 C6
Rose St. DA11 41 B2
Rosherville Way. DA11 41 D2
Rural Vale. DA11 41 D3
St Botolphs Rd. DA11 41 C6
St Thomas Rd. DA11 41 D5
Salem Rd. DA11 41 C3
Saunders Clo. DA11 41 D5
Saxon Clo. DA11 41 C6
Shepherd St. DA11 41 C3
South Kent Av. DA11 41 B2
Springhead Rd. DA11 41 C4
Station Rd. DA11 41 A2
Station Rd,
Spring Head. DA13 41 A6
Stonebridge Rd. DA11 41 A1
Tennyson Walk. DA11 41 C6
Thames Way. DA11 41 D3
The Creek. DA11 41 B1
The Hedgerows. DA11 41 C6
The Hill. DA11 41 C2
The Shore. DA11 41 C1
Third Av. DA11 41 D4
Tooley St. DA11 41 C3
Tudor Clo. DA11 41 D4
Vale Rd. DA11 41 C3
Vicarage Dri. DA11 41 C2
Viking Rd. DA11 41 C6
Wallis Pl. DA11 41 A1
Warwick Pl. DA11 41 B2
Waterdales. DA11 41 C5
Watling St. DA11 41 A5
West Kent Av. DA11 41 B2
Wingfield Bank. DA11 41 B5
Wombwell Gdns. DA11 41 D5
York Rd. DA11 41 C3

PADDOCK WOOD

Alliance Way. TN12 42 A4
Allington Rd. TN12 42 A3
Apple Ct. TN12 42 A4
Ashcroft Rd. TN12 42 B5
Badsell Rd. TN12 42 A5
Ballard Way. TN12 42 C3
Birch Rd. TN12 42 B4
Bowls Pl. TN12 42 B3
Bramley Gdns. TN12 42 A3
Bullfinch Clo. TN12 42 B5
Bullion Clo. TN12 42 C4
Catts Pl. TN12 42 D5
Chaffinch Way. TN12 42 C4
Challenger Clo. TN12 42 A4
Chantlers Hill. TN12 42 B6
Church Rd. TN12 42 B3
Claverdell Rd. TN12 42 B3
Cobbs Clo. TN12 42 A4
Cogate Rd. TN12 42 A4
Commercial Rd. TN12 42 B4
Concord Clo. TN12 42 A4
Court Hope. TN12 42 C3
Dimmock Clo. TN12 42 C3
Eastlands. TN12 42 A2
Eastwell Clo. TN12 42 A3
Eldon Way. TN12 42 B4
Ewins Clo. TN12 42 B4
Forest Rd. TN12 42 B3
Forge Way. TN12 42 B3
Fuggles Clo. TN12 42 A4
Goldfinch Clo. TN12 42 B5
Goldings. TN12 42 A5
Granary. TN12 42 C4
Haywain Clo. TN12 42 B5
Henley Rd. TN12 42 B3
Hop Pocket La. TN12 42 B3
Hornbeam Clo. TN12 42 B5
INDUSTRIAL ESTATES:
Eldon Way Ind Est. TN12 42 A3
Paddock Wood Dist Centre. TN12 42 C3
Transfesa. TN12 42 C3

Kent Clo. TN12 42 B4
Keyworth Clo. TN12 42 A4
Kiln Way. TN12 42 B5
Larch Gro. TN12 42 B5
Laxton Gdns. TN12 42 A3
Le Temple Rd. TN12 42 C4
Linden Clo. TN12 42 B5
Linnet Way. TN12 42 B5
Lucknow Rd. TN12 42 B3
Lucks La. TN12 42 C2
MacDonald Ct. TN12 42 B4
Maidstone Rd, Five Oak
 Green. TN12 42 A1
Maidstone Rd,
 Paddock Wood. TN12 42 A6
Mascalls Court Rd.
 TN12 42 A6
Mascalls Park. TN12 42 A5
Mercers Clo. TN12 42 A4
Mile Oak Rd. TN12 42 D6
Mount Pleasant. TN12 42 A4
New Rd. TN12 42 B4
Newton Gdns. TN12 42 A3
North Down Clo. TN12 42 B4
Nursery Rd. TN12 42 B3
Oaklea Rd. TN12 42 B3
Old Kent Rd. TN12 42 B4
Pearsons Green Rd.
 TN12 42 D5
Pinewood Clo. TN12 42 B4
Queen St. TN12 42 D5
Redpoll Walk. TN12 42 B5
Ribston Gdns. TN12 42 A3
Ringden Av. TN12 42 A5
Rowan Way. TN12 42 B5
St Andrews Clo. TN12 42 B4
St Andrews Rd. TN12 42 B4
Siskin Gdns. TN12 42 B5
Staces Cotts. TN12 42 B5
Station App. TN12 42 B3
Station Rd. TN12 42 B3
Sycamore Gdns. TN12 42 B5
The Bines. TN12 42 B5
The Cedars. TN12 42 B3
The Greenways. TN12 42 A5
The Ridings. TN12 42 B3
The Shires. TN12 42 C3
Transfesa Rd. TN12 42.B2
Tutsham Way. TN12 42 A4
Wagon La. TN12 42 C1
Walnut Clo. TN12 42 B4
Warrington Rd. TN12 42 B4
Woodlands. TN12 42 A3
Yeoman Gdns. TN12 42 A4

QUEENBOROUGH

Alsager Rd. ME11 43 A3
Argent Rd. ME11 43 B3
Barler Pl. ME11 43 C1
Bartletts Clo. ME12 43 D1
Borough Rd. ME11 43 C2
Brielle Way. ME11 43 C1
Castle St. ME11 43 B1
Castlemere Av. ME11 43 C1
Chalk Rd. ME11 43 B1
Coronation Cres. ME11 43 B1
Court Hall. ME11 43 A1
Cullet Dri. ME11 43 B3
Dumergue Av. ME11 43 C1
Eastern Av. ME11 43 C2
Edward Rd. ME11 43 A3
Ferry Way. ME11 43 A3
First Av. ME11 43 B3
Foxley Rd. ME11 43 B1
Georgian Clo. ME11 43 C3
Gordon Av. ME11 44 C1
Harold St. ME11 43 C1
High St. ME11 43 A1
Hillside Av. ME11 43 A3
INDUSTRIAL ESTATES:
Klondyke Ind Est.
 ME11 43 B2
Jubilee Cres. ME11 43 B1
Main Rd. ME11 43 C1
Manor Clo. ME11 43 B3
Manor Rd. ME11 43 B3
Marshall Cres. ME11 43 B3
Moat Way. ME11 43 C1
Mountfield. ME11 43 C1
North Rd. ME11 43 B1
Park Av. ME11 43 C2
Park Rd. ME11 43 A1
Queenborough Rd.
 ME12 43 D1

Railway Ter. ME11 43 B1
River View. ME11 43 B3
Rushenden Rd. ME11 43 B3
Second Av. ME11 43 B3
Sheet Glass Rd. ME11 43 B3
South St. ME11 43 B1
Stanley Av. ME11 43 C2
Sterling Rd. ME11 43 C1
Swale Av. ME11 43 A3
The Rise. ME12 43 D1
Uplands Way. ME12 43 D1
Well Rd,
 Rushenden. ME11 43 A3
Well Rd,
 Queenborough. ME11 43 B3
West St. ME11 43 A1
Wykeham Clo. ME11 43 B3
Yevele Clo. ME11 43 C1

RAINHAM

Absolam Ct. ME8 44 A2
Arthur Rd. ME8 44 B4
Ashley Rd. ME8 44 B4
Asquith Rd. ME8 44 A6
Balmer Clo. ME8 44 B5
Barleycorn Dri. ME8 44 C6
Beacon Clo. ME8 44 B5
Bedford Av. ME8 44 B3
Beechings Grn. ME8 44 A1
Beechings Way. ME8 44 A1
Begonia Av. ME8 44 A2
Bendon Way. ME8 44 B4
Berengrave La. ME8 44 C3
Bettescombe Rd. ME8 44 B5
Beverley Clo. ME8 44 D4
Birling Av. ME8 44 B3
Blean Rd. ME8 44 A2
Bodian Clo. ME8 44 B4
Bonnington Grn. ME8 44 A1
Boston Gdns. ME8 44 A3
Boughton Clo. ME8 44 B4
Bransgore Clo. ME8 44 B5
Broadview Av. ME8 44 C4
Brockenhurst Clo. ME8 44 B5
Broomcroft Rd. ME8 44 D2
Brown St. ME8 44 C3
Bushmeadow Rd. ME8 44 D2
Caldew Av. ME8 44 A3
Caledonian Ct. ME8 44 C4
Callans Clo. ME8 44 B6
Cambridge Rd. ME8 44 A6
Camellia Clo. ME8 44 B5
Caversham Clo. ME8 44 D3
Century Rd. ME8 44 B4
Chalfont Dri. ME8 44 B6
Chalky Bank Rd. ME8 44 D2
Charlotte Dri. ME8 44 A3
Cheriton Rd. ME8 44 B4
Cherry Amber Clo. ME8 44 D4
Cherry Tree Rd. ME8 44 A2
Chesham Dri. ME8 44 B6
Chestfield Clo. ME8 44 C2
Childscroft Rd. ME8 44 D2
Chilton Ct. ME8 44 C3
Cowbeck Clo. ME8 44 B6
Cozenton Cl. ME8 44 C3
Crabtree Rd. ME8 44 B4
Cranbrook Clo. ME8 44 A1
Cranford Clo. ME8 44 B3
Crundale Rd. ME8 44 A1
Danson Way. ME8 44 B4
De Mere Clo. ME8 44 B6
Deanwood Clo. ME8 44 B6
Deanwood Dri. ME8 44 B6
Denbigh Av. ME8 44 A3
Derwent Way. ME8 44 B4
Detling Clo. ME8 44 A2
Devon Clo. ME8 44 C3
Dignals Clo. ME8 44 D2
Doddington Rd. ME8 44 A1
Dorset Sq. ME8 44 B3
Durham Rd. ME8 44 A5
Eastling Clo. ME8 44 B1
Edwin Rd. ME8 44 B4
Elizabeth Ct. ME8 44 A2
Elmstone Rd. ME8 44 B5
Ely Clo. ME8 44 C2
Findlay Clo. ME8 44 B6
Fordwich Grn. ME8 44 A1
Frinsted Clo. ME8 44 A1
Gainsborough Clo.
 ME8 44 B6
Gayhurst Clo. ME8 44 B5

Gifford Clo. ME8 44 A1
Glistening Glade. ME8 44 C6
Glynne Clo. ME8 44 B6
Granary Clo. ME8 44 D3
Guardian Ct. ME8 44 A3
Hartpiece Clo. ME8 44 C2
Harvesters Clo. ME8 44 C5
Harvey Rd. ME8 44 B4
Hawthorne Av. ME8 44 A2
Henley Clo. ME8 44 B4
Herbert Rd. ME8 44 C4
Hereford Clo. ME8 44 B2
Herne Rd. ME8 44 B3
High Elms. ME8 44 C2
High St. ME8 44 C3
Highfield Clo. ME8 44 A5
Highfield Rd. ME8 44 B5
Holding St. ME8 44 C3
Hollingsbourne Rd.
 ME8 44 A1
Holmoaks. ME8 44 C2
Holtwood Clo. ME8 44 B6
Honeybee Glade. ME8 44 C6
Hothfield Rd. ME8 44 D3
Hudson Dri. ME8 41 A3
Hurst Pl. ME8 44 C4
Idenwood Clo. ME8 44 B6
Iversgate Clo. ME8 44 D2
Ivy St. ME8 44 D4
Jackson Clo. ME8 44 A3
Jefferson Dri. ME8 44 A3
Kendal Way. ME8 44 B4
Kenilworth Dri. ME8 44 B5
Kenilworth Gdns. ME8 44 B5
Lakewood Dri. ME8 44 A6
Lancaster Ct. ME8 44 A5
Langdale Clo. ME8 44 A3
Laurel Walk. ME8 44 C6
Lichfield Clo. ME8 44 B2
Lineacre Clo. ME8 44 B6
London Rd. ME8 44 A3
Longford Clo. ME8 44 D4
Longley Rd. ME8 44 C3
Lonsdale Dri. ME8 44 B6
Lower Bloors La. ME8 44 B3
Lower Rainham Rd.
 ME8 44 D1
Lyminge Clo. ME8 44 A3
Lyndhurst Av. ME8 44 A6
Maidstone Rd. ME8 44 A6
Maplins Clo. ME8 44 D3
Marshall Rd. ME8 44 B3
Mayfield Clo. ME8 44 C2
Medway Rd. ME8 44 D3
Megby Clo. ME8 44 B6
Meresborough Rd.
 ME8 44 D6
Miers Court Rd. ME8 44 C6
Milstead Rd. ME8 44 A1
Minster Rd. ME8 44 A1
Monmouth Clo. ME8 44 B2
Mossy Glade. ME8 44 C6
Napwood Clo. ME8 44 B6
Newnham Clo. ME8 44 A2
Nightingale Clo. ME8 44 C6
Norfolk Clo. ME8 44 B2
Norreys Rd. ME8 44 C5
Northumberland Av.
 ME8 44 C3
Nursery Rd. ME8 44 B4
Oldfield Clo. ME8 44 B4
Orchard St. ME8 44 C5
Parkfield Rd. ME8 44 B4
Patrixbourne Av. ME8 44 A2
Pembury Way. ME8 44 C2
Penshurst Clo. ME8 44 B2
Petham Grn. ME8 44 A1
Pikefields. ME8 44 A2
Ploughmans Way. ME8 44 C6
Pluckley Clo. ME8 44 B2
Preston Way. ME8 44 A2
Pudding Rd. ME8 44 D4
Pump La. ME8 44 A2
Quinnell St. ME8 44 B4
Ringwood Clo. ME8 44 B4
Ripon Clo. ME8 44 B2
River View. ME8 44 B1
Roberts Rd. ME8 44 B4
Rolvenden Av. ME8 44 A1
Romany Rd. ME8 44 A1
Roystons Clo. ME8 44 D2
Ruckinge Way. ME8 44 A1
Salisbury Av. ME8 44 B4
Sandhurst Clo. ME8 44 B4
Sandown Dri. ME8 44 B5
Scott Av. ME8 44 D4
Sellinge Grn. ME8 44 A1

Selsted Clo. ME8 44 A2
Shelden Dri. ME8 44 D4
Signal Ct. ME8 44 D3
Silverdale Rd. ME8 44 C5
Silverspot Clo. ME8 44 C5
Soloman Rd. ME8 44 D3
Springvale. ME8 44 A5
Station Rd. ME8 44 D3
Stratford Av. ME8 44 B4
Streetfield Rd. ME8 44 D3
Sturry Way. ME8 44 A2
Suffolk Av. ME8 44 D3
Suffolk Ct. ME8 44 D3
Sunningdale Clo. ME8 44 B6
Sunningdale Rd. ME8 44 B6
Sunnyfields Clo. ME8 44 C4
Sutherland Gdns. ME8 44 C6
Sutton Clo. ME8 44 D3
Sylvan Rd. ME8 44 A4
Tanker Hill. ME8 44 B6
Taverners Rd. ME8 44 B5
Tavistock Clo. ME8 44 C5
Thames Av. ME8 44 C4
The Crofters. ME8 44 D5
The Goldings. ME8 44 A4
The Mailyns. ME8 44 B5
The Old Orchard. ME8 44 D3
The Platters. ME8 44 A5
The Willows. ME8 44 C2
Thornham Rd. ME8 44 A1
Truro Clo. ME8 44 B1
Tudor Gro. ME8 44 C4
Tufton Rd. ME8 44 C2
Vancouver Dri. ME8 44 A3
Waltham Rd. ME8 44 A1
Waterworks La. ME8 44 A3
Webster Rd. ME8 44 D3
Wentworth Dri. ME8 44 B5
Wheatcroft Gro. ME8 44 B2
Whitegate Ct. ME8 44 B6
Wimbourne Dri. ME8 44 B4
Windermere Dri. ME8 44 B5
Wingham Clo. ME8 44 A1
Woodchurch Cres.
 ME8 44 A2
Woodpecker Glade.
 ME8 44 A6
Woodside. ME8 44 A6
Wooldeys Rd. ME8 44 D2
Wooton Grn. ME8 44 B1
Wright Clo. ME8 44 A2

RAMSGATE

Abbots Hill. CT11 45 B5
Addington Pl. CT11 45 B5
Addington St. CT11 45 A5
Adelaide Gdns. CT11 45 B5
Albert Rd. CT11 45 C4
Albert St. CT11 45 A5
Albion Hill. CT11 45 B5
Albion Pl. CT11 45 B5
Albion Rd. CT11 45 C4
Alexandra Rd. CT11 45 A3
Alma Pl. CT11 45 B4
Alma Rd. CT11 45 B3
Alpha Rd. CT11 45 A5
Anns Rd. CT11 45 B3
Archway Rd. CT11 45 B5
Argyle Dri. CT11 45 B2
Arklow Sq. CT11 45 C4
Artillery Rd. CT11 45 B4
Augusta Rd. CT11 45 C4
Avebury Av. CT11 45 C2
Avenue Rd. CT11 45 C4
Ayton Rd. CT11 45 A5
*Bailiemoor Ct,
 Argylle Rd. CT11 45 B2
Balmoral Pl. CT11 45 A5
Bay View Rd. CT10 45 C1
Beechcroft Gdns. CT11 45 C3
Belgrave Clo. CT11 45 A4
Bellevue Clo. CT11 45 A4
Bellevue Rd. CT11 45 A4
Belmont Rd. CT11 45 A4
Belmont St. CT11 45 B4
Beresford Rd. CT11 45 A5
Binnie Clo. CT10 45 C1
Bolton St. CT11 45 A3
Boughton Av. CT10 45 D1
Boundary Rd. CT11 45 A4
Briars Walk. CT11 45 C1
Brights Pl. CT11 45 B4
Broad St. CT11 45 B4
Brockenhurst Rd. CT11 45 C3

Brunswick St. CT11 45 B
Camden Sq. CT11 45 B
Cannon Rd. CT11 45 A
Cannonbury Rd. CT11 45 A
Carlton Av. CT11 45 A
Cavendish St. CT11 45 B
Cecilia Rd. CT11 45 B
Central Rd. CT11 45 A
Chapel Place La. CT11 45 A
Charles Rd. CT11 45 B
Chatham Pl. CT11 45 B
Chatham St. CT11 45 A
Church Hill. CT11 45 B
Church Rd. CT11 45 B
Clarendon Gdns. CT11 45 A
Cleaver La. CT11 45 B
Cliff St. CT11 45 B
Cliffside Dri. CT11 45 D
Clifton Lawn. CT11 45 A
Codrington Rd. CT11 45 A
Colburn Rd. CT10 45 D
College Rd. CT11 45 A
Cornhill. CT11 45 B
Cornwall Av. CT11 45 C
Coronation Rd. CT11 45 A
Cottage Rd. CT11 45 B
Cranbourne Clo. CT11 45 C
Crescent Rd. CT11 45 A
Cumberland Rd. CT11 45 A
D'este Rd. CT11 45 C
Dane Cres. CT11 45 B
Dane Park Rd. CT11 45 B
Dane Rd. CT11 45 B
Darren Gdns. CT10 45 B
Denmark Rd. CT11 45 B
Detling Av. CT10 45 D
Dumpton Gap Rd.
 CT10 45 D
Dumpton La. CT11 45 D
Dumpton Pk Dri. CT11 45 C
Dumpton Pk Rd. CT11 45 C
Duncan Rd. CT11 45 A
*Dunoon Ct,
 Argylle Dri. CT11 45 B
Eagle Hill. CT11 45 A
Effingham St. CT11 45 B
Elham Way. CT10 45 D
Elizabeth Rd. CT11 45 C
Ellen Av. CT11 45 B
Ellington Rd. CT11 45 A
Elmstone Rd. CT11 45 A
Elms Av. CT11 45 A
Ethelbert Rd. CT11 45 A
Fairfield Rd. CT11 45 A
Finsbury Rd. CT11 45 B
Flora Rd. CT11 45 B
Francis Gdns. CT10 45 C
Freda Clo. CT10 45 C
Fortuna Ct. CT11 45 A
George St. CT11 45 B
Gilbert Rd. CT11 45 B
Gordon Rd. CT11 45 A
Grange Rd. CT11 45 A
Grange Rd. CT11 45 A
Grange Way. CT10 45 C
*Granville Farm Mews,
 Thanet Rd. CT11 45 C
Grove Rd. CT11 45 A
Grundys Hill. CT11 45 A
Guildford Lawn. CT11 45 A
Harbour Par. CT11 45 B
Harbour St. CT11 45 B
Hardres Rd. CT11 45 B
,Hardres St. CT11 45 B
Harrison Rd. CT11 45 A
Hatfield Rd. CT11 45 A
Hawkhurst Way. CT10 45 D
Hawthorn Clo. CT11 45 A
Heathwood Dri. CT11 45 E
Hereson Rd. CT11 45 E
Hertford Pl. CT11 45 E
Hertford St. CT11 45 E
Hibernia St. CT11 45 E
High St. CT11 45 E
Hillbrow Rd. CT11 45 A
Hollicondane Rd. CT11 45 A
Holly Rd. CT11 45 E
Honeysuckle Rd. CT11 45 C
Irchester St. CT11 45 A
Ivy La. CT11 45 A
James St. CT11 45 A
Kent Pl. CT11 45 E
*Kilbride Ct,
 Argylle Dri. CT11 45 E
King St. CT11 45 E
Kings Rd. CT11 45 A
Lenham Clo. CT10 45 D
Leonards Av. CT11 45 E

eopold Rd. CT11 45 B3
eopold St. CT11 45 B5
Ilian Rd. CT11 45 C3
verpool Lawn. CT11 45 C3
yndhurst Rd. CT11 45 C3
adeira Walk. CT11 45 B5
argate Rd. CT10 45 A2
arina Esp. CT11 45 C5
arina Rd. CT11 45 C4
arlborough Rd. CT11 45 A5
eeting St. CT11 45 B4
ilitary Rd. CT11 45 B5
ichael Av. CT11 45 C3
ill Cotts. CT11 45 A5
inster Clo. CT11 45 D1
ontague Rd. CT11 45 B3
ontefiore Av. CT11 45 C2
ontefiore Cotts,
  Hereson Rd. CT11 45 C4
oss End Mews. CT11 45 B1
uir Rd. CT11 45 C2
ulberry Clo. CT11 45 B5
elson Cres. CT11 45 B5
ewcastle Hill. CT11 45 B4
ewlands La. CT11 45 A1
ewlands Rd. CT12 45 A2
icholls Av. CT10 45 C1
orth Av. CT11 45 A5
cean Vw. CT10 45 D2
Old Dairy Clo,
  Victoria Rd. CT11 45 C4
ackers La. CT11 45 B4
aradise. CT11 45 A4
aragon. CT11 45 A6
aragon St. CT11 45 A6
ark Av. CT10 45 B1
ark Chase. CT10 45 B1
ark Gate. CT10 45 B1
ark Rd. CT11 45 A4
arkwood Clo. CT10 45 A4
enshurst Rd. CT11 45 C4
ercy Rd. CT11 45 A3
lains of Waterloo.
  CT11 45 B4
oplar St. CT11 45 B5
restedge Av. CT11 45 B1
rinces Rd. CT11 45 A3
riory Rd. CT11 45 A5
romenade. CT10 45 C1
rospect Ter. CT11 45 B5
ueen St. CT11 45 B5
ueens Rd. CT11 45 C4
amsgate Rd. CT10 45 C1
chmond Rd. CT11 45 A5
odney St. CT11 45 A5
ose Hill. CT11 45 B5
osebery Av. CT11 45 C2
osemary Av. CT10 45 C1
osemary Gdns. CT10 45 C1
Rothsay Ct,
  Argyle Dri. CT11 45 B2
oyal Cres. CT11 45 A6
oyal Par. CT11 45 B5
oyal Rd. CT11 45 A5
t Andrews Rd. CT11 45 C3
t Augustines Rd. CT11 45 A6
t Benedicts Lawn.
  CT11 45 A5
St Catherines Ct,
  Argylle Dri. CT11 45 B2
t Davids Rd. CT11 45 C2
t Georges Rd. CT11 45 C3
t Lukes Av. CT11 45 A3
t Lukes Rd. CT11 45 B3
t Patricks Rd. CT11 45 C3
alisbury Av,
  Broadstairs. CT10 45 C1
alisbury Av,
  Ramsgate. CT11 45 B3
anctuary Clo. CT10 45 C1
andwood Rd. CT11 45 C2
chool La. CT11 45 B4
eacroft Rd. CT10 45 D1
even Stones Dri. CT10 45 D2
haftesbury St. CT11 45 A4
hah Pl. CT11 45 A4
herwood Gdns. CT11 45 B2
hirley Av. CT11 45 B5
ion Hill. CT11 45 B5
outh Cliff Par. CT10 45 B5
outh Eastern Rd. CT11 45 A4
pencer Sq. CT11 45 A5
pringfield Clo. CT11 45 B5
taffordshire St. CT11 45 B4
tanley Pl. CT11 45 B5
tanley Rd. CT11 45 A3
taplehurst Av. CT10 45 D1

Station Approach Rd.
  CT11 45 A3
Stonar Clo. CT11 45 B2
Sundew Gro. CT11 45 B3
Sussex St. CT11 45 B4
Sydney Rd. CT11 45 C3
Tavistock Rd. CT11 45 B2
Thanet Rd. CT11 45 C3
The Cloisters. CT11 45 A5
Thorn Gdns. CT11 45 B2
Tomsons Pass. CT11 45 A4
Townley St. CT11 45 B5
Trinity Pl. CT11 45 C4
Truro Rd. CT11 45 C4
Turner St. CT11 45 B4
Union Rd. CT11 45 C3
Union St. CT11 45 B4
Unity Pl. CT11 45 C4
Upper Dumpton
  Park Rd. CT11 45 B3
Vale Pl. CT11 45 A5
Vale Rd. CT11 45 A5
Vale Sq. CT11 45 A5
Vereth Rd. CT11 45 A5
Victoria Par. CT11 45 C4
Victoria Rd. CT11 45 C4
Vine Clo. CT11 45 B1
Waldron Rd. CT10 45 D1
Wallwood Rd. CT11 45 D1
Warten Rd. CT11 45 C2
Watchester Av. CT11 45 A6
Waterloo Pl. CT11 45 B4
Weatherly Dri. CT10 45 C1
Wellington Cres. CT11 45 C5
West Cliff Prom. CT11 45 A5
West Cliff Rd. CT11 45 A5
West Dumpton La.
  CT11 45 B1
Western Esp. CT10 45 D1
Wickham Av. CT11 45 C3
Willsons Rd. CT11 45 A5
Winstanley Cres. CT11 45 A3
Winterstoke Cres. CT11 45 C3
Winterstoke
  Undercliff. CT11 45 C4
Winterstoke Way. CT11 45 C3
Woodford Av. CT12 45 B5
York St. CT11 45 B5
York Ter. CT11 45 B5

ROCHESTER

Abbots Clo. ME1 46 B6
Albany Rd. ME1 46 C5
Albert Pl. ME2 46 C1
Albert Rd. ME1 46 C5
Alma Pl. ME2 46 B2
Almon La. ME1 46 B3
Amherst Rd. ME1 46 D5
Arthur Rd. ME1 46 A6
Ash Rd. ME2 46 A2
Backfields. ME1 46 C4
Baker St. ME1 46 C5
Bakers Walk. ME1 46 C3
Bardell Ter. ME1 46 D6
Barnaby Ter. ME1 46 D6
Barton Rd. ME2 46 B1
Beech Rd. ME2 46 A2
*Bishops Walk,
  Eastgate. ME1 46 D3
Blue Boar La. ME1 46 C3
Boley Hill. ME1 46 C3
Borstal Mews. ME1 46 A6
Borstal Rd. ME1 46 B5
Borstal St. ME1 46 A6
Bowes Rd. ME2 46 C1
Brambletree Cres. ME1 46 A6
Breton Rd. ME1 46 C6
Bridge Rd. ME1 46 C6
Brompton La. ME2 46 B1
Broom Hill Rd. ME2 46 A1
Bryant Rd. ME2 46 B2
Bull La. ME1 46 C2
Burgess Rd. ME2 46 C1
Burrit Mews. ME1 46 D5
Burritt St. ME1 46 C6
Cambria Av. ME1 46 A6
Canal Rd. ME2 46 D2
Canon Clo. ME1 46 C6
Carton Clo. ME1 46 D5
Castle Av. ME1 46 C5
Castle Hill. ME1 46 C2
Castle View Rd. ME1 46 A1
Catherine St. ME1 46 D5
Cavendish Rd. ME1 46 D5

Cazeneuve St. ME1 46 D4
Cecil Rd. ME1 46 D5
Cedar Rd. ME2 46 A3
Central Par. ME1 46 D6
Central Rd. ME2 46 A1
Chariot Way. ME2 46 A4
Charles St. ME2 46 B2
Church Path. ME2 46 B1
Church St. ME1 46 D4
City Way. ME1 46 D4
Clarence Av. ME1 46 D4
Clive Rd. ME1 46 D5
College Yd. ME1 46 C3
Commercial Rd. ME2 46 B2
Commissioners Rd.
  ME2 46 D1
Cookham Hill. ME1 46 B6
Copperfield Rd. ME1 46 D6
Cordelia Cres. ME1 46 A6
Cornwall Rd. ME1 46 C5
Corporation St. ME1 46 D2
Cossack St. ME1 46 D5
Cowdrey Clo. ME1 46 B4
Crossways. ME1 46 C5
Crow La. ME1 46 D3
Cuxton Rd. ME2 46 A3
Dale Rd. ME1 46 C6
Darnley Rd. ME2 46 A2
Dart Clo. ME2 46 A2
Delce Rd. ME1 46 D4
Dickens Rd. ME1 46 C6
Doggetts Sq. ME2 46 C2
Dombey Clo. ME1 46 D6
Dorritt Way. ME1 46 D6
Downside. ME2 46 A1
Dunnings La. ME1 46 D4
East Row. ME1 46 D3
Eastgate. ME1 46 D3
Eastgate Ct. ME1 46 D3
Eastgate Ter. ME1 46 D3
Eden Mews. ME1 46 D3
Edward St. ME2 46 B1
Elmtree Dri. ME1 46 B6
Epaul La. ME1 46 C2
Esplanade. ME1 46 B5
Ethelbert Rd. ME1 46 C4
Farmdale Av. ME1 46 A6
Foord St. ME1 46 D4
Fort St. ME1 46 D4
Friary Pl. ME1 46 C1
Frobisher Gdns. ME1 46 D3
Furrells Rd. ME1 46 D3
Galbri Dri. ME2 46 A2
Gashouse Rd. ME1 46 D2
George La. ME1 46 D3
Glanville Rd. ME2 46 B1
Gleanings Mews. ME1 46 C3
Glovers Mill. ME1 46 D5
Goddings Dri. ME1 46 B5
Gordon Rd. ME2 46 A1
Gordon Ter. ME1 46 C4
Grange Rd. ME2 46 C1
Grange Way. ME1 46 C5
Gravel Walk. ME1 46 D4
Gravesend Rd. ME2 46 A1
Grove Rd. ME2 46 C1
Gun La. ME2 46 B1
Gundulph Sq. ME1 46 C2
Hathaway Ct. ME1 46 C3
Havisham Clo. ME1 46 D6
Hawkwood Clo. ME1 46 D4
Hawthorn Rd. ME2 46 A2
*Hellyar Ct,
  John St. ME1 46 D4
Hever Croft. ME2 46 A3
High Bank. ME1 46 D6
High St,
  Rochester. ME1 46 C2
High St,
  Strood. ME2 46 B1
Hill Rd. ME1 46 B6
Hillside. ME1 46 B6
Holcombe Rd. ME1 46 C4
Hoopers Pl. ME1 46 D4
Hoopers Rd. ME1 46 D4
Horsewash La. ME1 46 C2
Horsley Rd. ME1 46 C6
Howard Av. ME1 46 D5
Humber Cres. ME1 46 A1
INDUSTRIAL ESTATES:
Ballard Business Pk.
  ME2 46 A3
Castle View Business
  Centre. ME1 46 D2
Fine Line Ind Est.
  ME2 46 D1
Nightingale Business
  Est. ME2 46 D1

Phoenix Ind Est. ME2 46 D1
Roman Way Ind Est.
  ME2 46 A4
Temple Ind Est. ME2 46 B2
James St. ME1 46 D4
Jasper Av. ME1 46 D6
Jenner Rd. ME1 46 D4
Jersey Rd. ME2 46 A1
John St. ME1 46 D4
King Edward Rd. ME1 46 C3
King St. ME1 46 C3
Kings Av. ME1 46 C5
Kings Orchard. ME1 46 D3
Kingswear Gdns. ME2 46 C1
Knight Rd. ME2 46 B2
La Providence. ME1 46 D3
Langdon Rd. ME1 46 C4
Laura Pl. ME1 46 A6
Lockington Gro. ME1 46 C3
London Rd. ME2 46 A1
Longley Rd. ME1 46 C4
Love La. ME1 46 C3
Magwitch Clo. ME1 46 B4
Maidstone Rd. ME1 46 C5
Malt Mews. ME1 46 C3
Manor La. ME1 46 A6
Mansell Dri. ME1 46 A6
Maple Rd. ME2 46 A2
Marley Way. ME1 46 D6
Marsh St. ME2 46 C1
May Rd. ME1 46 D5
Mercury Clo. ME1 46 B6
Miles Pl. ME1 46 D5
Minor Canon Row.
  ME1 46 C3
Mitre Rd. ME1 46 C4
Montfort Rd. ME2 46 B1
Morden St. ME1 46 C4
Mount Rd. ME1 46 B6
New Rd. ME1 46 D4
Newark Yd. ME2 46 C1
Nickleby Clo. ME1 46 D6
Norman Clo. ME2 46 A4
North Bank Clo. ME2 46 A3
North Gate. ME1 46 D2
North St. ME2 46 B1
Northcote Rd. ME2 46 A2
Oliver Twist Clo. ME1 46 C4
Onslow Rd. ME1 46 D5
Orange Ter. ME1 46 D4
Pepys Way. ME2 46 A1
Pickwick Cres. ME1 46 D6
Pine Rd. ME2 46 A2
Poplar Clo. ME2 46 A3
Poplar Rd. ME2 46 A3
Priestfields. ME1 46 B6
Princes St. ME1 46 B2
Queen St. ME1 46 B2
Rectory Grange. ME1 46 C6
Richard St. ME1 46 D5
Ridley Rd. ME1 46 C4
Roach St. ME2 46 B2
Rochester Av. ME1 46 C4
Roebuck Rd. ME1 46 C4
Roffen Rd. ME1 46 C4
Roman Way. ME2 46 A4
Rose St. ME1 46 D4
Ross St. ME1 46 D4
St Margarets Banks.
  ME1 46 D4
St Margarets Mews.
  ME1 46 C3
St Margarets St. ME1 46 C4
St Marys Rd. ME2 46 C1
St Matthews Dri. ME1 46 B6
St Nicholas Gdns. ME2 46 A1
St Peter St. ME1 46 D4
St Williams Way. ME1 46 D4
Saxon Pl. ME2 46 A4
Shaws Way. ME1 46 C4
Shorts Reach. ME1 46 C5
Shorts Way. ME1 46 C4
Sidney Rd. ME1 46 B6
Smith St. ME2 46 B2
South Eastern Rd. ME2 46 C1
Southfields. ME1 46 C4
Stanhope Rd. ME1 46 B1
Star Hill. ME1 46 D4
Station Rd. ME2 46 C1
Steerforth Clo. ME1 46 D6
Stirling Clo. ME1 46 B6
Sunderland Clo. ME1 46 B5
Swain Clo. ME2 46 A1
Tamar Dri. ME2 46 A2
Taylors La. ME1 46 B2
Temple Gdns. ME2 46 A2
The Close. ME1 46 C4

The Common. ME1 46 D2
The Mews. ME2 46 A2
The Queen Mother Ct.
  ME1 46 C4
The Rise. ME1 46 D6
The Terrace. ME1 46 D3
Thomas St. ME1 46 D5
Tintagel Clo. ME2 46 A2
Tintagel Gdns. ME2 46 A2
Tolgate La. ME2 46 A1
Tolgate Rd. ME1 46 C4
Two Post Alley. ME1 46 C2
Union St. ME1 46 D4
Vange Mews. ME1 46 C4
Vicarage Rd. ME1 46 B2
Victoria St,
  Rochester. ME1 46 D4
Victoria St,
  Strood. ME2 46 A4
Viking Clo. ME2 46 A4
Vines La. ME1 46 C3
Warblers Clo. ME2 46 B1
Warden Rd. ME1 46 C6
Warwick Cres. ME1 46 A6
Watling St. ME2 46 A1
Watts Av. ME1 46 A4
Weatherly Clo. ME1 46 D4
Weller Av. ME1 46 D6
Weston Av. ME2 46 A1
Wickham St. ME1 46 D5
Winford Mews. ME1 46 B6
Witham Way. ME2 46 A2
Whitewall Rd. ME2 46 D1
Whitewall Way. ME2 46 D1
Woodstock Rd. ME2 46 A1
Wyatt Pl. ME2 46 A1
Wykeham St. ME2 46 B1
York Rd. ME1 46 C5

ST MARGARETS at CLIFFE

Bay Hill. CT15 43 C6
Bay Hill Clo. CT15 43 C6
Beach Rd. CT15 43 C6
Cavenagh Rd. CT15 43 D5
Chapel La. CT15 43 B4
Churchill Clo. CT15 43 B6
Convent Clo. CT15 43 C5
Cripps La. CT15 43 B5
Dover Rd. CT15 43 A4
Downside. CT15 43 C5
Droveway Gdns. CT15 43 B5
Glebe Clo. CT15 43 A5
Granville Rd. CT15 43 C5
High St. CT15 43 B5
Hotel Rd. CT15 43 D5
Kenilworth Clo. CT15 43 C5
Kingsdown Rd. CT15 43 B4
Knotts La. CT15 43 B5
Langdon Clo. CT15 43 A6
Lighthouse Rd. CT15 43 C6
Long Steps. CT15 43 C6
Millfield. CT15 43 A4
Norman Rd. CT15 43 D4
Reach Clo. CT15 43 B5
Reach Mdw. CT15 43 B5
Reach Rd. CT15 43 B6
Roman Way. CT15 43 B6
Royston Gdns. CT15 43 B5
St Georges Pl. CT15 43 B5
St Margarets Rd. CT15 43 C6
Salisbury Rd. CT15 43 C5
Sea St. CT15 43 B5
Station Rd. CT15 43 B4
The Avenue. CT15 43 B4
The Crescent. CT15 43 C6
The Droveway. CT15 43 B5
The Freedown. CT15 43 B4
The Rise. CT15 43 D4
Townsend Farm Rd.
  CT15 43 A4
Upper Rd. CT15 43 A6
Vicarage La. CT15 43 B5
Victoria Av. CT15 43 D4
Well La. CT15 43 B5

SANDWICH

Ash Rd. CT13 47 A2
Aynsley Ct. CT13 47 C2
Barnes Ende Ct. CT13 47 C3
Bell La. CT13 47 C3

Black La. CT13 47 A5
Bowling Corner. CT13 47 B2
Bowling St. CT13 47 B2
Brightlingsea Rd. CT13 47 B4
Burch Av. CT13 47 B4
Cattle Mkt. CT13 47 B3
Church St. CT13 47 C3
Church St,
St Marys. CT13 47 B2
Cottage Row. CT13 47 B2
Coventon La. CT13 47 B6
Deal Rd. CT13 47 B6
Delf St. CT13 47 B2
Delfside. CT13 47 C4
Denny La. CT13 47 A3
Dover Rd. CT13 47 A6
Fisher St. CT13 47 C3
Fordwich Pl. CT13 47 B4
Galliard St. CT13 47 C3
Guildcourt La. CT13 47 B2
Harnet St. CT13 47 B3
Hastings Pl. CT13 47 B4
Hazelwood Mdw. CT13 47 B4
High St. CT13 47 C3
Hogs Corner. CT13 47 C3
Honfleur Rd. CT13 47 B4
Hythe Pl. CT13 47 C4
INDUSTRIAL ESTATES:
Sandwich Ind Est.
CT13 47 D2
Johns Green. CT13 47 A6
Jubilee Rd. CT13 47 B4
King St. CT13 47 C3
Knightrider St. CT13 47 C3
Laburnum Av. CT13 47 A4
Loop Ct Mews. CT13 47 B2
Loop St. CT13 47 B3
Love La. CT13 47 C3
Manwood Rd. CT13 47 C3
Mill Clo. CT13 47 A2
Millwall Pl. CT13 47 C3
Moat Sole. CT13 47 B3
Mulberry Field. CT13 47 B2
New Romney Pl. CT13 47 C4
New St. CT13 47 B3
Paradise Row. CT13 47 B2
Pondicherry La. CT13 47 C3
Potter St. CT13 47 C3
Poulders Gdns. CT13 47 A4
Poulders Rd. CT13 47 A4
Quay La. CT13 47 C3
Ramsgate Rd. CT13 47 C2
Richborough Rd. CT13 47 A1
St Andrews Lees. CT13 47 C4
St Barts Rd. CT13 47 A4
St Georges Lees. CT13 47 C4
St Georges Rd. CT13 47 C4
St Peters St. CT13 47 C3
Sandown Rd. CT13 47 C3
Sandwich By-Pass.
CT13 47 A6
Sandwood Rd. CT13 47 B4
Sarre Pl. CT13 47 B4
School Rd. CT13 47 B2
Short St. CT13 47 C3
Stonar Clo. CT13 47 C2
Stonar Gdns. CT13 47 C2
Stone Cross Lees. CT13 47 B5
Stour St. CT13 47 B3
Strand St. CT13 47 B2
Sunnyside Gdns. CT13 47 A4
The Bulwark. CT13 47 C3
The Butchery. CT13 47 C2
The Causeway. CT13 47 B2
The Chain. CT13 47 C3
The Crescent. CT13 47 A6
The Quay. CT13 47 C3
Upper Strand St. CT13 47 C3
Vicarage La. CT13 47 B2
Wantsum Mews. CT13 47 B2
Wantsume Lees. CT13 47 A1
Watts St. CT13 47 B3
Whitefriars Mdw. CT13 47 B3
Whitefriars Way. CT13 47 B3
Woodnesborough Rd.
CT13 47 A5

SEVENOAKS

Akehurst La. TN13 48 C6
Allotment La. TN13 48 C3
Amherst Rd. TN13 48 B3
Argyle Rd. TN13 48 B5
Ashley Clo. TN13 48 B4
Ashley Rd. TN13 48 B4

Avenue Rd. TN13 48 C4
Bank St. TN13 48 B5
Bat & Ball Rd. TN14 48 B1
Bayham Rd. TN13 48 C3
Beech Rd. TN13 48 B5
Bethel Rd. TN13 48 C3
Birch Clo. TN13 48 B3
Blackhall La. TN15 48 D3
Blair Dri. TN13 48 B3
Blighs Rd. TN13 48 B5
Bosville Av. TN13 48 A3
Bosville Dri. TN13 48 A3
Bosville Rd. TN13 48 A3
Bouchier Clo. TN13 48 B6
Bradbourne Park Rd.
TN13 48 A3
Bradbourne Rd. TN13 48 B2
Bradbourne Vale Rd.
TN13 48 A2
Brewery La. TN13 48 B5
Buckhurst Av. TN13 48 B5
Buckhurst La. TN13 48 B5
Camden Rd. TN13 48 B2
Carrick Dri. TN13 48 B3
Cavendish Av. TN13 48 A2
Cedar Ter Rd. TN13 48 A3
Chancellor Way. TN13 48 A2
Charter House Dri.
TN13 48 A3
Chartway. TN13 48 C4
Chatham Hill Rd. TN13 48 B1
Chestnut La. TN13 48 B4
Clarendon Rd. TN13 48 A5
Clockhouse La. TN13 48 A3
Cobden Rd. TN13 48 C3
Coombe Av. TN14 48 B1
Cramptons Rd. TN14 48 B1
Crownfields. TN13 48 B6
Dartford Rd. TN13 48 C3
Dorset St. TN13 48 B5
Eardley Rd. TN13 48 A5
Egdean Walk. TN13 48 B3
Emily Jackson Clo.
TN13 48 A4
Farm Rd. TN14 48 C1
Filmer La. TN14 48 D1
Garden Rd. TN13 48 C2
Garvock Dri. TN13 48 A6
Golding Rd. TN13 48 B2
Gordon Rd. TN13 48 A5
Granville Rd. TN13 48 A4
Greatness La. TN14 48 C1
Greatness Rd. TN14 48 C1
Grove Rd. TN14 48 C1
Harrison Way. TN13 48 A2
Hartslands Rd. TN13 48 C3
High St. TN13 48 B5
Hill Crest. TN13 48 B4
Hillborough Av. TN13 48 D3
Hillingdon Av. TN13 48 C2
Hillingdon Rise. TN13 48 C2
Hillside Rd. TN13 48 B3
Hitchen Hatch La. TN13 48 A4
Holly Bush Clo. TN13 48 C4
Holly Bush La. TN13 48 C4
Holly Bush La. TN13 48 C3
Hollyoake Ter. TN13 48 A4
Holmesdale Rd. TN13 48 C3
Hospital Rd. TN13 48 C2
Hunsdon Dri. TN13 48 B4
Kennedy Gdns. TN13 48 C3
Kincraig Dri. TN13 48 A4
Kippington Rd. TN13 48 A5
Kirk Ct. TN13 48 A3
Knole La. TN13 ?8 C6
Knole Rd. TN13 48 C3
Knole Way. TN13 48 C5
Knotts Pl. TN13 48 A4
Lambarde Dri. TN13 48 A3
Lambarde Rd. TN13 48 A2
Lansdowne Rd. TN13 48 C3
Lime Tree Walk. TN13 48 B5
Linden Chase Rd. TN13 48 A3
Little Wood. TN13 48 C2
Locks Yard. TN13 48 B5
London Rd. TN13 48 B5
Lyle Park. TN13 48 B3
Meadow Clo. TN13 48 A3
Merlewood. TN13 48 A3
Mill La. TN13 48 C1
Mill Pond Clo. TN14 48 C1
Morel Ct. TN13 48 B5
Mount Harry Rd. TN13 48 A4
Nicholson Way. TN13 48 C3
Northview Rd. TN14 48 C1
Nursery Rd. TN13 48 C2
Oak Hill. TN13 48 A4

Oak Hill Rd. TN13 48 A5
Oak La. TN13 48 B6
Oak Sq. TN13 48 B6
Oakdene Rd. TN13 48 A3
Oakfields. TN13 48 B6
Oakwood Dri. TN13 48 B4
Orchard Clo. TN14 48 C1
Otford Rd. TN14 48 B1
Park La. TN13 48 B4
Pembroke Rd. TN13 48 B5
Pendennis Rd. TN13 48 B3
Pine Needle La. TN13 48 B3
Pinehurst. TN14 48 D1
Pinewood Av. TN14 48 D1
Plymouth Dri. TN13 48 B5
Plymouth Park. TN13 48 C5
Pound La. TN13 48 B4
Prospect Rd. TN13 48 C3
Quaker Clo. TN13 48 C3
Quakers Hall La. TN13 48 C3
Quarry Hill. TN15 48 D3
Queens Dri. TN14 48 C1
Rectory La. TN13 48 B6
Rockdale Rd. TN13 48 B6
Rose Field. TN13 48 A4
Sackville Clo. TN13 48 B2
St Botolphs Av. TN13 48 A4
St Botolphs Rd. TN13 48 A4
St Georges Rd. TN13 48 B2
St James Rd. TN13 48 B2
St Johns Hill. TN13 48 B2
St Johns Rd. TN13 48 B2
Sandy La. TN13 48 C3
Seal Hollow Rd. TN13 48 C4
Seal Rd. TN14 48 C1
Serpentine Ct. TN13 48 C3
Serpentine Rd. TN13 48 C3
Six Bells La. TN13 48 B6
South Park. TN13 48 A5
Station Par. TN13 48 A4
Suffolk Way. TN13 48 B5
Swaffield Rd. TN13 48 C2
The Crescent. TN13 48 D2
The Dene. TN13 48 B6
The Drive. TN13 48 B4
The Glade. TN13 48 B3
The Green. TN13 48 C4
The Paddocks. TN13 48 C4
The Shambles. TN13 48 B5
The Vine. TN13 48 B4
Thicketts. TN13 48 B3
Tubs Hill. TN13 48 A4
Tubs Hill Par. TN13 48 A4
Valley Dri. TN13 48 B5
Victoria Rd. TN13 48 B5
View Rd. TN13 48 A3
Vine Av. TN13 48 B4
Vine Court Rd. TN13 48 B4
Warren Ct. TN13 48 B5
Weavers La. TN14 48 C1
Webbs Alley. TN13 48 C6
Well Ct. TN13 48 B3
Westfield. TN13 48 C2
White Lodge Clo. TN13 48 B4
Wickenden Rd. TN13 48 D2
Wilderness Mt. TN13 48 D2
Wildernesse Av. TN15 48 D2
Winchester Gro. TN13 48 A4
Wood Lodge Grange.
TN13 48 B2
Woodland Rise. TN15 48 D3
Woodside Rd. TN13 48 A3
Yeomans Mdw. TN13 48 A6

SHEERNESS

Acorn St. ME12 49 D3
Albion Pl. ME12 49 D3
Alder Clo. ME12 49 B5
Alma Rd. ME12 49 D3
Almond Tree Clo. ME12 49 B5
Anchor La. ME12 49 B1
Appledore Av. ME12 49 C5
Archway Rd. ME12 49 B2
Beach St. ME12 49 C2
Berridge Rd. ME12 49 D3
Bonetta Ct. ME12 49 C4
Botany Clo. ME12 49 D3
Boxley Clo. ME12 49 C5
Bredhurst Clo. ME12 49 C5
Bridge Rd. ME12 49 C2
Bridgewater Rd. ME12 49 A5
Brielle Way. ME12 49 A5
Briton Ct. ME12 49 C4
Broad St. ME12 49 C3

Broadway. ME12 49 D2
Carlton Av. ME12 49 C4
Cavour Rd. ME12 49 D3
Cecil Av. ME12 49 C4
Chapel St. ME12 49 B2
Charles St. ME12 49 B2
Cherry Tree Clo. ME12 49 B5
Chilham Clo. ME12 49 C5
Clarence Row. ME12 49 D2
Coats Av. ME12 49 B5
Coronation Rd. ME12 49 A3
Cromwell Rd. ME12 49 B5
Cross St. ME12 49 C2
Davie Clo. ME12 49 B5
Delamark Rd. ME12 49 D2
Detling Clo. ME12 49 C5
Diamond Ct. ME12 49 C4
Dock Rd. ME12 49 B1
Dorset Rd. ME12 49 B4
East La. ME12 49 B2
Edenbridge Dri. ME12 49 C5
Esplanade. ME12 49 C2
Estuary Rd. ME12 49 C3
First Av. ME12 49 D3
Fleet Av. ME12 49 C3
Fonblanque Rd. ME12 49 C4
Galway Rd. ME12 49 D3
Grace Rd. ME12 49 B3
Granville Pl. ME12 49 D3
Granville Rd. ME12 49 C3
Hare St. ME12 49 C2
Harris Rd. ME12 49 D3
Hartlip Clo. ME12 49 C5
Hawthorn Av. ME12 49 B5
High St,
Blue Town. ME12 49 B2
High St,
Mile Town. ME12 49 C2
Holland Clo. ME12 49 C3
Hope St. ME12 49 C3
Invicta Rd. ME12 49 D3
Kent Rd. ME12 49 C4
Kent St. ME12 49 B2
King St. ME12 49 B2
Kings Head Alley.
ME12 49 B2
Larch Ter. ME12 49 B5
Linden Dri. ME12 49 B5
Main Rd. ME12 49 B2
Maple St. ME12 49 D4
Medway Rd. ME12 49 C3
Meyrick Rd. ME12 49 D2
Milstead Clo. ME12 49 C5
Miranda Ct. ME12 49 C4
Montague Ct. ME12 49 C4
Nelson Clo. ME12 49 B4
New Rd. ME12 49 B4
New St. ME12 49 C3
Newcomen Rd. ME12 49 D2
Newland Rd. ME12 49 B5
Pepys Av. ME12 49 A6
Pier Rd. ME12 49 C2
Portland Ter. ME12 49 D3
Queens Way. ME12 49 B5
Railway Rd. ME12 49 C2
Ranelagh Rd. ME12 49 D2
Regents Pl. ME12 49 D2
Rose St. ME12 49 C3
Royal Rd. ME12 49 D2
Rule Ct. ME12 49 C4
Russell St. ME12 49 C4
St Agnes Gdns. ME12 49 D4
St Georges Av. ME12 49 C4
St Georges Ct. ME12 49 C4
School La. ME12 49 B2
Second Av. ME12 49 D3
Shearwater Ct. ME12 49 C4
Sheppey St. ME12 49 B2
Short St. ME12 49 C2
Shrubsole Av. ME12 49 D3
South Vw Gdns. ME12 49 D4
Strode Cres. ME12 49 C3
Swale Av. ME12 49 C3
Thames Av. ME12 49 C4
Tribune Ct. ME12 49 C4
Trinity Pl. ME12 49 D2
Trinity Rd. ME12 49 D2
Turners Clo. ME12 49 C4
Union St. ME12 49 B2
Victoria St. ME12 49 D4
Victory St. ME12 49 C4
Vincent Gdns. ME12 49 D3
West La. ME12 49 B2
West Rd. ME12 49 B2
Wheatsheaf Gdns.
ME12 49 C4
Whiteway Rd. ME12 49 A6

Winstanley Rd. ME12 49
Wood St. ME12 49

SITTINGBOURNE

Addington Rd. ME10 50
Adelaide Dri. ME10 50
Albany Rd. ME10 50
All Saints Rd. ME10 50
Ambleside. ME10 50
Arthur St. ME10 50
Ashington Clo. ME10 50
Aubretia Walk. ME10 50
Avenue of
Remembrance. ME10 50
Balmoral Ter. ME10 50
Barkers Ct. ME10 50
Barrow Gro. ME10 50
Bassett Rd. ME10 50
Bayford Rd. ME10 50
Beaconsfield Rd. ME10 50
Bell Rd. ME10 50
Belmont Rd. ME10 50
Berkeley Ct. ME10 50
Berry St. ME10 50
Blenheim Rd. ME10 50
Blythe Clo. ME10 50
Bonham Dri. ME10 50
Borden La. ME10 50
Bourne Gro. ME10 50
Bracken Ct. ME10 50
Bradley Dri. ME10 50
Brenchley Rd. ME10 50
Broom Rd. ME10 50
Burley Rd. ME10 50
Burnup Bank. ME10 50
Caldew Gro. ME10 50
Cambridge Rd. ME10 50
Canterbury Rd. ME10 50
Capel Rd. ME10 50
Castle Rd. ME10 50
Cavell Way. ME10 50
Cedar Clo. ME10 50
Central Av. ME10 50
Chalkwell Rd. ME10 50
Charlotte St. ME10 50
Chartwell Gro. ME10 50
Chaucer Rd. ME10 50
Chilton Av. ME10 50
Church Rd. ME10 50
Church St,
Milton Regis. ME10 50
Church St. ME10 50
Clover Ct. ME10 50
Cobham Av. ME10 50
College Rd. ME10 50
Commonwealth Clo.
ME10 50
Connaught Rd. ME10 50
Coombe Dri. ME10 50
Cowper Rd. ME10 50
Cremers Rd. ME10 50
Crescent St. ME10 50
Crown Quay La. ME10 50
Crown Rd. ME10 50
Dalewood. ME10 50
Dickson Ct. ME10 50
Does All. ME10 50
Dolphin Rd. ME10 50
Dover St. ME10 50
Downs Clo. ME10 50
Eagles Clo. ME10 50
East St. ME10 50
Eastwood Rd. ME10 50
Elm Gro. ME10 50
Epps Rd. ME10 50
Eurolink Way. ME10 50
Fairleas. ME10 50
Fairview Rd. ME10 50
Falcon Ct. ME10 50
Fallowfield. ME10 50
Farm Cres. ME10 50
Fern Walk. ME10 50
Fernleigh Ter. ME10 50
Fielder Clo. ME10 50
Fountain St. ME10 50
Frederick St. ME10 50
Frensham Clo. ME10 50
Fulston Pl. ME10 50
Gas Rd. ME10 50
Gayhurst Dri. ME10 50
Gaze Hill Av. ME10 50
George St. ME10 50
Gerrards Dri. ME10 50
Gibson St. ME10 50

ebe La. ME10 50 E3
overs Cres. ME10 50 C3
odnestone Rd. ME10 50 E2
ore Court Rd. ME10 50 B4
orse Rd. ME10 50 F1
afton Rd. ME10 50 D2
afton Way. ME10 50 D2
amlins Ct. ME10 50 A3
ayshott Clo. ME10 50 D3
eenways. ME10 50 F3
anover Clo. ME10 50 C4
arkness Ct. ME10 50 F2
arold Rd. ME10 50 E2
arrier Dri. ME10 50 E4
arris Gdns. ME10 50 F1
arvey Dri. ME10 50 D4
awthorn Rd. ME10 50 B1
aysel. ME10 50 D4
eard Way. ME10 50 E1
eather Clo. ME10 50 D2
gh St,
Milton Regis. ME10 50 C1
gh St,
Sittingbourne. ME10 50 C2
ghstead Rd. ME10 50 C3
ll Brow. ME10 50 A3
obart Gdns. ME10 50 A2
ome View. ME10 50 F2
omewood Av. ME10 50 A2
oneysuckle Ct. ME10 50 F1
ugh Price Clo. ME10 50 F1
ythe Rd. ME10 50 B1
IDUSTRIAL ESTATES:
Eurolink Ind Centre.
ME10 50 D2
London Rd
Trading Est. ME10 50 B2
hnson Rd. ME10 50 B2
bilee St. ME10 50 B1
enilworth Ct. ME10 50 A1
ent Av. ME10 50 A3
estrel Clo. ME10 50 D3
eswick Av. ME10 50 F2
in Clo. ME10 50 D3
ng St. ME10 50 C1
ngsmill Clo. ME10 50 B2
iburnum Pl. ME10 50 B2
insdowne Rd. ME10 50 F2
ivender Ct. ME10 50 D3
me Gro. ME10 50 D2
nden Clo. ME10 50 A3
ttle Glovers. ME10 50 C3
ndon Rd. ME10 50 A2
ngridge. ME10 50 E4
dbrook Clo. ME10 50 A2
ndhurst Gro. ME10 50 B4
anor Gro. ME10 50 B3
anwood Clo. ME10 50 C4
edway Clo. ME10 50 B2
eeres Ct La. ME10 50 F1
erlin Clo. ME10 50 D3
ddle Way. ME10 50 F3
ll Ct. ME10 50 E3
ll Way. ME10 50 C1
llen Rd. ME10 50 B1
llfield. ME10 50 D3
lton Rd. ME10 50 C2
nterne Av. ME10 50 A4
uddy La. ME10 50 E4
urston Rd. ME10 50 E2
orthwood Dri. ME10 50 C4
atfields. ME10 50 E3
ak Rd. ME10 50 F1
ast Ct. ME10 50 C4
chard Pl. ME10 50 E3
sprey Ct. ME10 50 E3
rk Av. ME10 50 B4
rk Dri. ME10 50 B4
rk Rd. ME10 50 B3
mbury St. ME10 50 C2
nn Clo. ME10 50 F4
regrine Dri. ME10 50 D3
riwinkle Clo. ME10 50 B1
nd Dri. ME10 50 D3
rtland Av. ME10 50 F2
ulsen Ct. ME10 50 F2
ince Charles Av.
ME10 50 F3
ctory Rd. ME10 50 E3
gency Ct. ME10 50 B1
ddles Rd. ME10 50 A3
verhead Clo. ME10 50 A3
ck Rd. ME10 50 B2
man Sq. ME10 50 C2
mney Ct. ME10 50 B1
onagh Ct. ME10 50 B4
seleigh Rd. ME10 50 A4
St Johns Av. ME10 50 F3
St Michaels Clo. ME10 50 D2
St Michaels Rd. ME10 50 C2
St Pauls St. ME10 50 B1
School Rd. ME10 50 E3
Shakespeare Rd. ME10 50 E2
Shortlands Rd. ME10 50 E2
Shurland Av. ME10 50 C4
Silverdale Gro. ME10 50 A3
Smeed Clo. ME10 50 F2
South Av. ME10 50 D3
Springfield Rd. ME10 50 A1
Stanhope Av. ME10 50 D3
Staple Clo. ME10 50 B1
Staplehurst Rd. ME10 50 B1
Station Pl. ME10 50 C2
Station St. ME10 50 C2
Step Style. ME10 50 F4
Sterling Rd. ME10 50 A4
Sunny Bank. ME10 50 F1
Swan Clo. ME10 50 E2
Swanstree Av. ME10 50 E4
Sydney Av. ME10 50 A2
Symonds Dri. ME10 50 E1
Tavistock Clo. ME10 50 A2
Temple Gdns. ME10 50 E3
Terrace Rd. ME10 50 E2
The Burrs. ME10 50 D3
The Butts. ME10 50 D2
The Fairway. ME10 50 C4
The Fieldings. ME10 50 C4
The Finches. ME10 50 D3
The Forum. ME10 50 C2
The Meadows. ME10 50 C4
The Mews. ME10 50 C3
The Roundel. ME10 50 C4
The Wall. ME10 50 C1
Thistle Walk. ME10 50 F1
Thomas Rd. ME10 50 E2
Thorn Walk. ME10 50 F1
Tonge Rd. ME10 50 F2
Ufton La. ME10 50 B3
Unity St. ME10 50 B3
Upper Field Rd. ME10 50 E1
Valenciennes Rd. ME10 50 B3
Victoria Rd. ME10 50 A2
Vincent Rd. ME10 50 F3
Viners Clo. ME10 50 C4
Wadham Pl. ME10 50 E4
Walmer Gdns. ME10 50 B1
Walnut Tree Clo. ME10 50 A2
Warren Clo. ME10 50 F4
Waterloo Rd. ME10 50 A1
Watling Pl. ME10 50 E3
Watsons Hill. ME10 50 B1
Weald Ct. ME10 50 B4
Well Winch Rd. ME10 50 A1
West La. ME10 50 E2
West Ridge. ME10 50 B3
West St. ME10 50 B2
Westbourne St. ME10 50 C2
Westerham Rd. ME10 50 A3
Wharf Way. ME10 50 C1
Wheatcroft Clo. ME10 50 F2
Whitehall Rd. ME10 50 B4
William St. ME10 50 B2
Windermere Gro.
ME10 50 A3
Windsor Dri. ME10 50 A4
Woodbury Dri. ME10 50 F2
Woodcourt Clo. ME10 50 B4
Woodlands Rd. ME10 50 E3
Woodside Gdns. ME10 50 A4
Woodstock Rd. ME10 50 B4
Wykeham Rd. ME10 50 F2

SNODLAND

Annie Rd. ME6 51 B4
Apple Clo. ME6 51 C4
Ashbee Clo. ME6 51 C3
Auden Rd. ME20 51 C6
Austen Way. ME20 51 B6
Barrie Dri. ME20 51 B6
Bates Clo. ME20 51 C6
Bellingham Rd. ME20 51 D6
Betjeman Clo. ME20 51 B6
Bingley Clo. ME6 51 B2
Birling Rd. ME6 51 B3
Blake Dri. ME20 51 B6
Bramley Rd. ME6 51 C2
Bronte Clo. ME20 51 B6
Brook La. ME6 51 B4
Brook Rd. ME20 51 B6
Brook St. ME6 51 D2
Brookfield Av. ME20 51 C6
Brooklands Rd. ME20 51 C6
Browning Clo. ME20 51 B6
Bull Fields. ME6 51 C2
Busbridge Rd. ME6 51 A3
Cemetery Rd. ME6 51 B1
Chapel Rd. ME6 51 C2
Charles Clo. ME6 51 C2
Chaucer Way. ME20 51 C6
Chesterton Rd. ME20 51 B6
Christie Dri. ME20 51 B6
Church Field. ME6 51 D1
Clock Tower Mews.
ME6 51 C1
Coleridge Clo. ME20 51 B6
Constitution Hill. ME6 51 B1
Coombe Clo. ME6 51 C3
Cooper Rd. ME6 51 B4
Corona Ter. ME6 51 B4
Covey Hall Rd. ME6 51 C1
Coxs Clo. ME6 51 B2
Cronin Clo. ME20 51 B6
Delamere Gdns. ME6 51 C1
Dowling Clo. ME6 51 B2
Dryland Rd. ME6 51 B2
East St. ME6 51 D2
Freelands Rd. ME6 51 B2
Gassons Rd. ME6 51 A2
Gighill Rd. ME20 51 B6
Godden Rd. ME6 51 B2
Gorham Clo. ME6 51 B2
*Hammonds Sq,
Rocfort Rd. ME6 51 C2
Hendy Rd. ME6 51 D1
High St. ME6 51 C2
Hodgson Cres. ME6 51 C1
Holborough Rd. ME6 51 C2
Hollow La. ME6 51 B3
Hook Rd. ME6 51 B2
INDUSTRIAL ESTATES:
Industrial Dist. Centre.
ME6 51 B4
Mid Kent Business
Centre. ME6 51 D3
Larkfield Trading Est.
ME20 51 D5
Jerome Rd. ME20 51 B6
Kent Rd. ME6 51 C3
Kipling Dri. ME20 51 B6
Lakeside View. ME6 51 B4
Lakeview Clo. ME6 51 C4
Lambert Mews. ME6 51 C1
Lee Rd. ME6 51 C1
Leybourne Way. ME20 51 A6
Lucus Rd. ME6 51 A3
Lunsford La. ME20 51 B6
Macaulay Clo. ME20 51 B6
Malling Rd. ME6 51 B4
Marlowe Rd. ME20 51 B6
Marsh Way. ME20 51 C6
Masefield Way. ME20 51 B6
May St. ME6 51 D2
Meadow Walk. ME6 51 B2
Midsummer Rd. ME6 51 A2
Mill La. ME6 51 D2
Mill St. ME6 51 D2
Morhen Clo. ME6 51 B3
Nevill Pl. ME6 51 C3
Nevill Rd. ME6 51 C3
New Hythe La. ME20 51 D6
Norman Rd. ME6 51 C3
Orchard Way. ME6 51 B3
Orwell Clo. ME20 51 B6
Ostlers Ct. ME6 51 C2
Oxford St. ME6 51 C2
Paddlesworth Rd. ME6 51 A1
Papyrus Rd. ME20 51 D6
Portland Pl. ME6 51 C2
Pout Rd. ME6 51 B3
Pridmore Rd. ME6 51 B2
Queens Av. ME6 51 C1
Queens Rd. ME6 51 C2
Recreation Av. ME6 51 C2
Rectory Clo. ME6 51 C2
Ritch Rd. ME6 51 A2
River Way. ME20 51 C6
Roberts Rd. ME6 51 B2
Rocfort Rd. ME6 51 C2
Roman Rd. ME6 51 B2
St Benedict Rd. ME6 51 A3
St Katherines La. ME6 51 B3
Saltings Rd. ME6 51 C3
Sandy La. ME6 51 A3
Sassoon Clo. ME20 51 C6
Sharnal La. ME6 51 C3
Simpson Rd. ME6 51 C4
Snodland By-Pass.
ME6 51 C1
Snodland Rd. ME6 51 A3
Sort Mill Rd. ME6 51 D3
Southey Way. ME20 51 B6
Springfield Rd. ME20 51 A6
Stevens Clo. ME6 51 C2
Stevenson Way. ME20 51 B6
Taylor Rd. ME6 51 B2
The Groves. ME6 51 B3
Thomson Clo. ME6 51 C1
Tilghman Way. ME6 51 D1
Tom Joyce Clo. ME6 51 B3
Tomlin Clo. ME6 51 C2
Townsend Rd. ME6 51 A2
Vauxhall Cres. ME6 51 C4
Veles Rd. ME6 51 B2
Waghorn Rd. ME6 51 C2
Watts Clo. ME6 51 D1
Westmead. ME20 51 D5
Whitedyke Rd. ME6 51 A1
Willowside. ME6 51 C1
Woodlands Av. ME6 51 B1
Wordsworth Way.
ME20 51 C6
Wyvern Clo. ME6 51 B3

SOUTHBOROUGH

All Saints Rd. TN4 52 C6
Andrew Rd. TN4 52 D4
Argyle Rd. TN4 52 C2
Barnetts Clo. TN4 52 D4
Barnetts Way. TN4 52 D4
Bedford Rd. TN4 52 B4
Beltring Rd. TN4 52 B6
Birchwood Av. TN4 52 A2
Bounds Oak Way. TN4 52 A1
Breedon Av. TN4 52 B3
Brian Cres. TN4 52 C4
Brightridge. TN4 52 A4
Brokes Way. TN4 52 D4
Brookhurst Gdns. TN4 52 A2
Broomhill Pk Rd. TN4 52 A4
Cambrian Rd. TN4 52 D5
Carville Av. TN4 52 B3
Castle Rd. TN4 52 B2
Charles St. TN4 52 B4
Chestnut Av. TN4 52 C4
Chestnut Clo. TN4 52 C4
Church Rd. TN4 52 A2
Colebrook Rd. TN4 52 D5
Colonels Way. TN4 52 C3
Constitution Hill Rd.
TN4 52 A3
Crendon Park. TN4 52 B4
Crundwell Rd. TN4 52 A3
Cunningham Rd. TN4 52 C5
Darnley Dri. TN4 52 A1
Denbigh Rd. TN4 52 D6
Doon Brae. TN4 52 C2
Doric Av. TN4 52 B3
Doric Clo. TN4 52 B3
Dower House Cres.
TN4 52 A2
Draper St. TN4 52 B2
Dynevor Rd. TN4 52 D5
East Cliff Rd. TN4 52 C6
Edward St. TN4 52 B3
Elm Rd. TN4 52 B4
Fairlight Clo. TN4 52 C2
Fernhurst Cres. TN4 52 C2
Forge Rd. TN4 52 B4
Garlinge Rd. TN4 52 B3
Gordon Rd. TN4 52 D5
Great Bounds Dri. TN4 52 A1
Great Brooms Rd. TN4 52 D4
Grosvenor Rd. TN4 52 D6
Harlands Way. TN4 52 A1
High Brooms Rd. TN4 52 D5
Highfield Rd. TN4 52 D5
Hill Crest. TN4 52 C4
Hill Garth. TN4 52 C5
Holden Corner. TN4 52 A3
Holden Park Rd. TN4 52 B4
Holden Rd. TN4 52 A3
Holmewood Rd. TN4 52 D5
Hopwood Gdns. TN4 52 C6
Horizon Clo. TN4 52 D4
Hythe Clo. TN4 52 B3
Impala Gdns. TN4 52 C6
Keel Gdns. TN4 52 A4
Kibbles La. TN4 52 A4
Ladys Gift Rd. TN4 52 A4
Laurel Bank. TN4 52 C5
Leighton Clo. TN4 52 B6
Little Bounds Clo. TN4 52 A1
London Rd. TN4 52 A1
Manor Rd. TN4 52 A3
Meadow Rd. TN4 52 B3
Mereworth Rd. TN4 52 C6
Merrion Clo. TN4 52 D6
Merrion Way. TN4 52 D6
Montgomery Rd. TN4 52 C5
New England Rd. TN4 52 C6
Newlands Rise. TN4 52 C6
Newlands Rd. TN4 52 C6
Newlands Way. TN4 52 C5
Norstead Gdns. TN4 52 C5
North Farm Rd. TN4 52 D5
Norton Rd. TN4 52 B3
Nursery Rd. TN4 52 D5
Oak End Clo. TN4 52 C3
Park House Gdns. TN4 52 B3
Park Rd. TN4 52 B3
Pennington Pl. TN4 52 C2
Pennington Rd. TN4 52 B2
Pinewood Gdns. TN4 52 B3
Powdermill Clo. TN4 52 D4
Powdermill La. TN4 52 C5
Prospect Pk. TN4 52 A3
Prospect Rd. TN4 52 B3
Reynolds La. TN4 52 A6
Riddlesdale Av. TN4 52 C6
Ruscombe Clo. TN4 52 B3
St Andrews Park Rd.
TN4 52 B3
St Davids Rd. TN4 52 C6
St Johns Pk. TN4 52 B4
St Johns Rd. TN4 52 C5
St Lukes Rd. TN4 52 D6
St Michaels Rd. TN4 52 C6
Salisbury Rd. TN4 52 D4
Sheffield Rd. TN4 52 B3
Silverdale La. TN4 52 D6
Silverdale Rd. TN4 52 D6
Sir Davids Park. TN4 52 A4
Smythe Clo. TN4 52 A1
South View Rd. TN4 52 D5
Southfield Rd. TN4 52 B6
Southfields Way. TN4 52 C5
Southwood Av. TN4 52 C6
Speldhurst Rd. TN4 52 A4
Springfield Rd. TN4 52 B3
Stephens Rd. TN4 52 C6
Stewart Rd. TN4 52 D5
Summerhill Av. TN4 52 B3
Taylor St. TN4 52 B4
Tedder Rd. TN4 52 C5
The Crescent. TN4 52 A1
The Fairways. TN4 52 C5
The Ridgeway. TN4 52 C4
Upper Dunstan Rd.
TN4 52 C6
Vale Av. TN4 52 B3
Vale Rd. TN4 52 B3
Valley Vw. TN4 52 C3
Vauxhall La. TN4 52 A1
Vicarage Rd. TN4 52 B2
Victoria Rd. TN4 52 A3
Weare Rd. TN4 52 D4
Welbeck Av. TN4 52 D5
West Park Av. TN4 52 B3
Western Rd. TN4 52 B4
Whitegate Clo. TN4 52 B4
Wilman Rd. TN4 52 C6
Wolseley Rd. TN4 52 D5
Woodland Rd. TN4 52 D5
Woodlands Clo. TN4 52 D5
Wooley Clo. TN4 52 A4
Wooley Rd. TN4 52 A4
Yew Tree Rd. TN4 52 B4

STAPLEHURST

Allen Sq. TN12 53 C3
Bathurst Clo. TN12 53 B3
Bathurst Rd. TN12 53 B3
Bell La. TN12 53 B4
Benden Clo. TN12 53 C3
Bower Walk. TN12 53 B3
Brooks Clo. TN12 53 B2
Butcher Clo. TN12 53 B3
Chapel La. TN12 53 C4
Chestnut Av. TN12 53 B3
Church Grn. TN12 53 B4
Clapper La. TN12 53 A2
Cork La. TN12 53 A6
Corner Farm Rd. TN12 53 B2
Cornforth Clo. TN12 53 C3
Crowther Clo. TN12 53 B3
Fir Tree Clo. TN12 53 C4

Fishers Clo. TN12 53 C2
Fishers Rd. TN12 53 C2
Fletcher Rd. TN12 53 B4
Frittenden Rd. TN12 53 C5
George St. TN12 53 A1
Goudhurst Rd. TN12 53 A6
Green Ct. TN12 53 B4
Gybbon Rise. TN12 53 B3
Hallwards. TN12 53 B5
Hanmer Way. TN12 53 B5
Headcorn Rd. TN12 53 C3
High St. TN12 53 C3
Hurst Clo. TN12 53 C2
Iden Cres. TN12 53 B5
Jaggard Way. TN12 53 B4
Jeffery Clo. TN12 53 A3
Kirkman Ct. TN12 53 B4
Knowles Walk. TN12 53 C3
Lindridge La. TN12 53 A1
Lodge Rd. TN12 53 B2
Lynhurst La. TN12 53 A5
McCabe Clo. TN12 53 B4
Maidstone Rd. TN12 53 B1
Marden Rd. TN12 53 A2
Marian Sq. TN12 53 C3
Market St. TN12 53 C1
Newlyn Dri. TN12 53 C2
North Down. TN12 53 B2
Offens Dri. TN12 53 B4
Oliver Rd. TN12 53 B3
Pinnock La. TN12 53 A5
Pope Dri. TN12 53 B3
Poyntell Rd. TN12 53 C3
Reeves Clo. TN12 53 B3
School La. TN12 53 C3
Slaney Rd. TN12 53 C3
South Bank. TN12 53 B4
Stanley Clo. TN12 53 A3
Staple Dri. TN12 53 C3
Station App. TN12 53 B1
Station Rd. TN12 53 B1
Surrenden Rd. TN12 53 B3
Sweetlands La. TN12 53 C1
Thatcher Rd. TN12 53 B3
The Parade. TN12 53 B4
The Quarter. TN12 53 B5
Tomlin Clo. TN12 53 B2
Usborne Clo. TN12 53 B4
Vine Walk. TN12 53 B4
Watkins Clo. TN12 53 B2
Weavers Clo. TN12 53 C3
Weld Clo. TN12 53 C3
Willow Cres. TN12 53 C1
Winchs Garth. TN12 53 C1

STROOD

Abbey Rd. ME2 54 A3
Albert Pl. ME2 54 D4
Allington Dri. ME2 54 A3
Alma Pl. ME2 54 C4
Ash Rd. ME2 54 B5
Ashenden Clo. ME2 54 D1
Bakers Walk. ME1 54 D5
Banks Rd. ME2 54 D3
Banning St. ME2 54 C3
Barton Rd. ME2 54 C4
Beaufort Rd. ME2 54 A3
Beech Rd. ME2 54 A5
Berber Rd. ME2 54 C3
Bill Street Rd. ME2 54 D2
Bingham Rd. ME2 54 D2
Boley Hill. ME1 54 D6
Bowes Rd. ME2 54 D3
Bramley Rise. ME2 54 A3
Brasted Ct. ME2 54 C2
Brompton Farm Rd. ME2 54 B2
Brompton La. ME2 54 C3
Broom Hill Rd. ME2 54 B3
Bryant Rd. ME2 54 C3
Burgess Rd. ME2 54 D4
Burleigh Clo. ME2 54 A3
Cadnum Clo. ME2 54 A4
Cambridge Rd. ME2 54 C3
Canal Rd. ME2 54 D4
Carrisbrooke Rd. ME2 54 A3
Castle Hill. ME1 54 D5
Castle View Rd. ME2 54 B4
Cecil Av. ME2 54 D3
Cedar Rd. ME2 54 A5
Central Rd. ME2 54 B4
Chapter Rd. ME2 54 A4
Charles St. ME2 54 C4
Chartwell Clo. ME2 54 D2
Chatsworth Dri. ME2 54 D2
Chequers Ct. ME2 54 B2
Chestnut Rd. ME2 54 A5
Church Grn. ME2 54 D3
Church Path. ME2 54 D4
Clarendon Gdns. ME2 54 C2
Cliffe Rd. ME2 54 C2
Clifton Clo. ME2 54 A5
Cobham Clo. ME2 54 A4
Collis St. ME2 54 C3
Columbine Clo. ME2 54 A4
Columbine Rd. ME2 54 A4
Commercial Rd. ME2 54 C4
Commissioners Rd. ME2 54 D3
Conway Clo. ME2 54 A2
Cooling Rd. ME2 54 D1
*Cranmere Ct, Vicarage Rd. ME2 54 D3
Crispin Rd. ME2 54 A3
Cromer Rd. ME2 54 C3
Cross St. ME2 54 C3
Cuxton Rd. ME2 54 B6
Daffodil Rd. ME2 54 A4
Darnley Rd. ME2 54 A5
Dart Clo. ME2 54 B5
Deacon Clo. ME2 54 A3
Dean Rd. ME2 54 A4
Dillywood La. ME3 54 A2
Doggetts Sq. ME2 54 D4
Dongola Rd. ME2 54 C3
Downside. ME2 54 B4
Drakes Av. ME2 54 B3
Duchess Clo. ME2 54 A3
Edward St. ME2 54 C4
Elaine Av. ME2 54 A4
Esplanade, Rochester. ME1 54 D6
Esplanade, Strood. ME2 54 D5
Everest La. ME2 54 C2
Farm Hill Av. ME2 54 B2
Florence St. ME2 54 D3
Fountain Rd. ME2 54 A2
Friary Pl. ME2 54 D4
Frindsbury Rd. ME2 54 D3
Galahad Av. ME2 54 A5
Galbri Dri. ME2 54 B5
Gardenia Clo. ME2 54 D1
Glanville Rd. ME2 54 C4
Gleaning Mews. ME2 54 D6
Goddington Rd. ME2 54 C3
Godfrey Clo. ME2 54 B2
Goldsworth Ct. ME2 54 C2
Gordon Rd. ME2 54 B4
Gorse Rd. ME2 54 B3
Grange Rd. ME2 54 D4
Grasmere Gro. ME2 54 D2
Gravesend Rd. ME2 54 A2
Grove Rd. ME2 54 D3
Gun La. ME2 54 C4
Hancock Clo. ME2 54 C2
Harlech Clo. ME2 54 A2
Harvel Av. ME2 54 A4
Hatfield Rd. ME2 54 C3
Hathaway Ct. ME1 54 D6
Hawthorn Rd. ME2 54 A5
Hayward Av. ME2 54 C3
Hever Croft. ME2 54 B6
High St. ME2 54 C4
Hillside Av. ME2 54 D3
Hilltop Rd. ME2 54 D2
Hillyfield Clo. ME2 54 B2
Holly Rd. ME2 54 A6
Hollywood La. ME3 54 D1
Hone St. ME2 54 C3
Honeypot Clo. ME2 54 D3
Humber Cres. ME2 54 B4
Hyperion Clo. ME2 54 B2
Iden Rd. ME2 54 D2
INDUSTRIAL ESTATES:
Temple Ind Est. ME2 54 C5
Jersey Rd. ME2 54 B4
King Arthurs Dri. ME2 54 B2
King Edward Rd. ME2 54 D6
Kingswear Gdns. ME2 54 D4
Kitchener Rd. ME2 54 C3
Knight Rd. ME2 54 B6
Laburnum Rd. ME2 54 A6
Lancelot Av. ME2 54 A5
Lancelot Clo. ME2 54 A5
Larkin Clo. ME2 54 D1
Leybourne Rd. ME2 54 A3
Lilac Rd. ME2 54 A6
Lingley Dri. ME2 54 D1
Linwood Av. ME2 54 A3
London Rd. ME2 54 B4
Love La. ME1 54 D6
Lower Rochester Rd. ME3 54 C1
Lychfield Dri. ME2 54 C2
Lyle Clo. ME2 54 C3
Lynette Av. ME2 54 C2
Lynors Av. ME2 54 C2
Malt Mews. ME1 54 D6
Maple Rd. ME2 54 B5
Marsh St. ME2 54 D4
Martin Rd. ME2 54 C3
Mayfair Clo. ME2 54 D2
Merryfields. ME2 54 C2
Mill Clo. ME2 54 D3
Mill Rd. ME2 54 C2
Millpond Clo. ME2 54 D3
Minerva Rd. ME2 54 C3
Montfort Rd. ME2 54 C4
Moore St. ME2 54 C3
Morland Dri. ME2 54 C2
Newark St. ME2 54 D4
North Bank Clo. ME2 54 B6
North St. ME2 54 C4
Northcote Rd. ME2 54 B5
Oak Rd. ME2 54 A5
Orchard Av. ME2 54 B3
Peckham Clo. ME2 54 D3
Pepys Way. ME2 54 B4
Pilgrims Way. ME2 54 B6
Pine Rd. ME2 54 B5
Poplar Clo. ME2 54 B6
Poplar Rd. ME2 54 A6
Povey Av. ME2 54 D1
Powlett Rd. ME2 54 D2
Priory Rd. ME2 54 C5
Prospect Av. ME2 54 D3
Quixote Cres. ME2 54 C2
Randolph Cotts. ME2 54 D2
* Rasi Clo, Powlett Rd. ME2 54 D2
Ravenswood Av. ME2 54 D3
Rede Court Rd. ME2 54 A3
Richborough Dri. ME2 54 C2
River Dri. ME2 54 A4
Roach St. ME2 54 C4
Roebuck Rd. ME1 54 D6
Rosemount Ct. ME2 54 B2
Russett Clo. ME2 54 A3
St Margarets Mws. ME1 54 D6
St Margarets St. ME1 54 D6
St Marys Rd. ME2 54 D4
*St Michaels Ct, Vicarage Rd. ME2 54 D3
St Nicholas Gdns. ME2 54 B4
Sandycroft Rd. ME2 54 B2
Saxon Clo. ME2 54 B2
Sherbourne Dri. ME2 54 C2
Slatin Rd. ME2 54 C3
Smetham Gdns. ME2 54 C2
Smith St. ME2 54 C5
South Eastern Rd. ME2 54 D4
Stanhope Rd. ME2 54 C4
Station Rd. ME2 54 D3
Steele St. ME2 54 C3
Stonehorse Ct. ME3 54 C1
Stonehorse La. ME3 54 C1
Stour Clo. ME2 54 A4
Swain Clo. ME2 54 B3
Sycamore Rd. ME2 54 A6
Tamar Dri. ME2 54 B5
Taylors La. ME2 54 D4
Temple Gdns. ME2 54 B5
The Mews. ME2 54 B4
Thirlmere Clo. ME2 54 D2
Tintagel Clo. ME2 54 B4
Tintagel Gdns. ME2 54 B5
Tolgate La. ME2 54 C4
Vicarage Rd. ME2 54 D3
Victoria St. ME1 54 D4
Vines La. ME1 54 D6
Warblers Clo. ME2 54 C4
Watermill Clo. ME2 54 D3
Watling St. ME2 54 A4
Weavering Clo. ME2 54 D1
West St. ME2 54 D2
Westergate Rd. ME2 54 B2
Weston Rd. ME2 54 C4
Willow Rd. ME2 54 A5
Windmill Clo. ME2 54 D2
Windmill St. ME2 54 C2
Witham Way. ME2 54 B4
Woodstock Rd. ME2 54 B4
Woodview Rise. ME2 54 B2
Worcester Clo. ME2 54 A3
Wyatt Pl. ME2 54 B4
Wykeham St. ME2 54 C3
Yalding Clo. ME2 54 D2

SWANLEY

Abbotts Clo. BR8 55 D4
Acacia Walk. BR8 55 A2
Alder Way. BR8 55 A2
Alexandra Clo. BR8 55 C2
Almond Dri. BR8 55 A2
Apple Orchard. BR8 55 A4
Archer Way. BR8 55 D2
Ash Clo. BR8 55 A2
Aspen Clo. BR8 55 A1
Azalea Dri. BR8 55 B4
Bartholomew Way. BR8 55 C3
Beech Av. BR8 55 D4
Best Ter. BR8 55 A5
Bevan Pl. BR8 55 C4
Birchwood Park Av. BR8 55 C3
Birchwood Rd. BR8 55 A1
Bonney Way. BR8 55 C2
Bourne Way. BR8 55 A3
Bramley Clo. BR8 55 B4
Bremner Clo. BR8 55 D4
Broadway. BR8 55 A6
Brook Rd. BR8 55 A3
Cedar Clo. BR8 55 A2
Charnock. BR8 55 C4
Cherry Av. BR8 55 A4
Church Farm Clo. BR8 55 A6
Church Rd. BR8 55 A6
Church View. BR8 55 B3
College Rd. BR8 55 B1
Conifer Way. BR8 55 A1
Court Cres. BR8 55 C4
Cranleigh Dri. BR8 55 C4
Cray Rd. BR8 55 A6
Crescent Gdns. BR8 55 A2
Cyclamen Rd. BR8 55 A4
Dahlia Dri. BR8 55 D2
Dale Rd. BR8 55 A2
Downsview Clo. BR8 55 C2
Edgar Clo. BR8 55 C3
Edward Gdns. BR8 55 B4
Egerton Av. BR8 55 C1
Ellis Clo. BR8 55 A4
Elm Dri. BR8 55 B2
Everest Pl. BR8 55 B4
Eynsford Rd. BR8 55 A6
Farm Av. BR8 55 A3
Five Wents. BR8 55 D2
Garrolds Clo. BR8 55 B2
Glendale. BR8 55 C5
Goldsel Rd. BR8 55 A5
Green Court Rd. BR8 55 A6
Greenacre Clo. BR8 55 B4
Greenside. BR8 55 A2
Hart Dyke Cres. BR8 55 A3
Hart Dyke Rd. BR8 55 A3
Harvest Wy. BR8 55 A1
Haven Clo. BR8 55 C2
Hazel End. BR8 55 C5
*Heath Clo, Sycamore Dri. BR8 55 B3
Heather End. BR8 55 B5
Heathfield Ter. BR8 55 A2
Heathwood Gdns. BR8 55 A2
Hewitt Pl. BR8 55 B4
Hibbs Clo. BR8 55 A2
High Firs. BR8 55 C4
High St. BR8 55 C4
Highlands Hill. BR8 55 D2
Hilda May Av. BR8 55 B2
Hillside Ct. BR8 55 D4
Hollytree Av. BR8 55 B2
Homefield Clo. BR8 55 C3
Irving Way. BR8 55 A2
Juniper Walk. BR8 55 B2
*Kennett Ct, Oakleigh Clo. BR8 55 B3
Kettlewell Ct. BR8 55 C2
Kingswood Av. BR8 55 C4
Laburnum Av. BR8 55 A3
Ladds Way. BR8 55 A4
Larch Walk. BR8 55 B2
Lavender Hill. BR8 55 A3
Lawn Clo. BR8 55 A2
Leechcroft Av. BR8 55 C3
Leewood Pl. BR8 55 A4
Lesley Clo. BR8 55 B3
Leydenhatch La. BR8 55 A1
Leyhill Clo. BR8 55 B4
Lilac Gdns. BR8 55 B3
Lilac Pl. BR8 55 B4
Lime Rd. BR8 55 B3
London Rd. BR8 55
Lower Croft. BR8 55
Lullingstone Av. BR8 55
Lynden Way. BR8 55
Main Rd, Crockenhill. BR8 55
Main Rd, Hextable. BR8 55
Manse Way. BR8 55
Maple Clo. BR8 55
Mark Way. BR8 55
Mayes Clo. BR8 55
Mead Clo. BR8 55
Millbro. BR8 55
*Montague Clo, St Georges Rd. BR8 55
Morello Clo. BR8 55
Moreton Clo. BR8 55
Moultain Hill. BR8 55
New Barn Rd. BR8 55
New Rd. BR8 55
Nightingale Way. BR8 55
Northview. BR8 55
Nursery Clo. BR8 55
Nutley Clo. BR8 55
Oakleigh Clo. BR8 55
Old Chapel Rd. BR8 55
Old Farm Gdns. BR8 55
Oliver Rd. BR8 55
Over Mead. BR8 55
Park Rd. BR8 55
Pear Tree Clo. BR8 55
Pemberton Gdns. BR8 55
Phillip Av. BR8 55
Pine Clo. BR8 55
Pinks Hill. BR8 55
Pioneer Way. BR8 55
Reeves Cres. BR8 55
Rogers Ct. BR8 55
Rowan Rd. BR8 55
Russet Way. BR8 55
Ruxton Clo. BR8 55
St Georges Rd. BR8 55
St Lukes Clo. BR8 55
St Marys Rd. BR8 55
Salisbury Av. BR8 55
Selah Dri. BR8 55
Sermon Dri. BR8 55
Seven Acres. BR8 55
Sheridan Clo. BR8 55
Shurlock Av. BR8 55
Sounds Lodge. BR8 55
Southern Pl. BR8 55
Southview Clo. BR8 55
Springfield Av. BR8 55
Spruce Dale Clo. BR8 55
Squires Field. BR8 55
Station App. BR8 55
Station Rd. BR8 55
Stone Cross Rd. BR8 55
Strawberry Fields. BR8 55
Stuart Clo. BR8 55
Swanley By Pass. BR8 55
Swanley La. BR8 55
Sycamore Dri. BR8 55
The Birches. BR8 55
The Croft. BR8 55
The Green. BR8 55
The Grove. BR8 55
The Oaks. BR8 55
The Orchard. BR8 55
The Spinney. BR8 55
Victoria Hill Rd. BR8 55
Walnut Way. BR8 55
Wansbury Way. BR8 55
Waterton. BR8 55
Waylands. BR8 55
West Harold. BR8 55
West View Rd. BR8 55
West View Rd, Crockenhill. BR8 55
Wested La. BR8 55
White Croft. BR8 55
Whiteoak Ct. BR8 55
Willow Av. BR8 55
Wisteria Gdns. BR8 55
Wood End. BR8 55
Woodgers Gro. BR8 55
Woodlands Clo. BR8 55
Woodlands Rise. BR8 55
Woodview Rd. BR8 55

TENTERDEN/ ST MICHAELS

Adams Clo. TN30 56
Admirals Walk. TN30 56

TONBRIDGE

TUNBRIDGE WELLS